Advanced Pressure Point Fighting of RYUKYU KEMPO

by George Dillman with Chris Thomas

Dillman Theory for all Systems

A Dillman Karate International Book

First published in 1994 by:
George Dillman Karate International
251 Mountain View Rd. (Grill)
Reading, PA 19607
U.S.A.

A NOTE TO THE READER

The ideas, techniques, and beliefs expressed in this book
are the result of years of study and practice. The knowledge
contained within is a synthesis of training which was obtained from
martial arts experts over a period of three decades. I realize and
understand that other persons are teaching similar theories,
and I commend their efforts at disseminating this vital information.
At the same time, I urge the reader to scrutinize the credentials
and depth of knowledge of all martial arts instructors before
assimilating those ideas into one's personal self-defense systems.
**Please use restraint when practicing all techniques contained
within this book. Practice only under supervision
of a qualified instructor.**

In memory...

So glad that our paths crossed...

World leaders in the martial arts, people I especially felt
close to–learned from–loved and miss...
        Bruce Lee
        Hohan Soken
        Robert Trias
        Ed Parker
        Daniel K. Pai

—George A. Dillman

The famous Bruce Lee and George Dillman together in 1967. "It was Bruce Lee who gave me hand speed, and I helped him with weapons." states George Dillman.

Acknowledgements

We would like to gratefully acknowledge and thank the many people who have made this book possible. Thanks go to Ed Lake, Dave Poirier, Jason Poirier, Lloyd Brown and Bill Burch for appearing in the pictures. An additional thanks to Bill Burch for making a special trip to help with a second photo shoot. Thanks to Ian Waite for appearing on the cover.

Thanks to Wendy Countryman, Tom Countryman and Kim Dillman for principle photography, and to Doug Churchill for the cover photography. Thanks to Sergio Onaga for his layout and cover design.

A special thanks to the many DKI instructors around the world, who are not only working hard to promote the spread of kyusho-jitsu, but who are contributing greatly to our understanding of the art through their own research and study. Also, our appreciation goes to all the school owners and instructors who have organized George Dillman seminars in their areas. Because of their efforts many thousands of martial artists have had the opportunity to experience first hand what kyusho-jitsu is all about.

Finally our sincerest thanks and highest respects to the many masters who have so freely shared knowledge with us over the years, especially Hohan Soken, Daniel K. Pai, Seiyu Oyata, Wally Jay and Remy Presas. It is our fervent hope that this contribution to the martial arts will reflect favorably on them.

Dedication

This work is gratefully dedicated to my family, Wendy, Josh, and April, and to my teachers, George Dillman, Steve Young and Robert Fusaro.

—Chris Thomas

"The depth and accuracy of the medical information in your book, <u>Advanced Pressure Point Fighting</u>, is unparalleled among current martial arts literature. Very Impressive."

-- Charles M. Terry, IV, M.D.
Philadelphia, PA

"An important, extremely practical book of self-defense, ... Accuracy, knowledge, grace, swiftness are necessary-- not strength or firepower."

-- The Book Reader, *Summer 1994*
(over 900 book stores carry The Book Reader)

" ... for a person not medically trained, Dillman's knowledge of anatomy and physiology is truly astounding."

-- Lois Buschbacher, M.D.
Indianapolis, IN

"Thank you for renewing my confidence in kata. ... Its an honor to have you as an instructor and a friend."

-- Ken Moreno, *Illinois stunt man / Movie actor*

" Dillman's meticulous presentation of muscle and nerve anatomy... has clarified the relationship of the Oriental theory of chi flow to modern anatomy and physiology as it relates to the martial arts. ... He has documented, scientifically, the important effects of carefully choosing targets for hand and foot strikes. ...This book should be an essential addition to the library of any serious martial artist. It is destined to become a classic."

-- Vincent C. Giampapa, M.D.
Asst' Clinical Prof., U.M.D.N.J.

"Dillman's first book was a sensation... Here's the sequel."

-- Terry O'Neill, *Fighting Arts International,*
England

"Dillman knows the musculoskeletal system better than some physicians."

-- Ralph Buschbacher, M.D.
Indianapolis, IN

" Thoroughly enjoyed it... I immediately came home and reached for my physiology textbook. I appreciate your sharing your knowledge with me."

-- Dr. David Ellis, D.C.
Washington, DC

" I truly believe you have unlocked the mystery in "bunkai". I commend you on your research and thank you for sharing it with karateka at large."

-- William J. Smith, Ph. D.
Boston, MA

1997 - George A. Dillman and members of Dillman Karate International did a medical study at a major university on pressure point attacks . . . here Dr. Chas Terry catches Ed Lake.

George and Kimberly Dillman on tour (1991) stop in at the original "Hard Rock" Cafe, London, England 20th anniversary celebration.
Photo by Leon Jay.

George A. Dillman in Queenstown, New Zealand (1991) standing in front of "Wicked Willies".
Photo by S. C. Chan.

Having fun in Scotland: George A. Dillman wears the kilts proudly on his largest seminar tour—fifteen countries around the world (Germany to Australia).
Photo by Kim Dillman, 1991.

Feb. 1993 family photo. Both sons have been doing karate since age 2. George IV and Allen were held as babies by the late Bruce Lee and Ed Parker. From left to right: Allen B. Dillman; George A. Dillman, III; George A. Dillman IV. *Photo by Kim Dillman.*

All grown up: George A. Dillman, III instructs his son George, IV in the art of karate as the three repose the 1970 photo from the book *Kyusho-jitsu—The Dillman Method of Pressure Point Fighting.* On the floor taking the punch is the youngest Dillman, Allen (age 28). *Photo by Kim Dillman, Feb. '93.*

George A. Dillman, IV does a Nai Hanchi move on brother Allen B. Dillman.
Photo by Kim Dillman, Feb. '93.

Paybacks on big brother can be fun! Allen B. Dillman does a Nai Hanchi attack on George IV.
Photo by Kim Dillman, Feb. '93.

George A. Dillman, 9th Degree Black Belt and Kimberly F. Dillman, 8th Degree Black Belt

A photo of real grand masters of the martial arts (left to right): Remy Presas, 10th Dan; George A. Dillman (author), 9th Dan; Wally Jay, 10th Dan; Jack Hogan, 8th Dan.

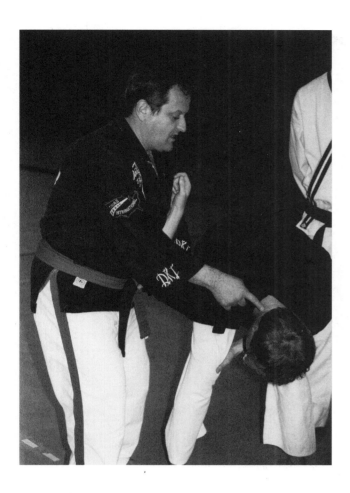

Members of DKI pose in front of a boxing statue in New Orleans, LA. Left to right: Hideki Frazier, CA; Carl Daigrepont, LA; George Dillman, PA; and Ron Richards, PA.

George Dillman shows a seminar crowd where to strike with a "Down Block" action after an arm trap from the most basic forms.
Photo by Kim Dillman.

George A. Dillman still flexible at age 51.

George Dillman, knocks out Lloyd Brown with a touch! These three seminar photos shot by Kim Dillman demonstrate the knockout and resuscitation. You must know how to restore energy properly to do these techniques...

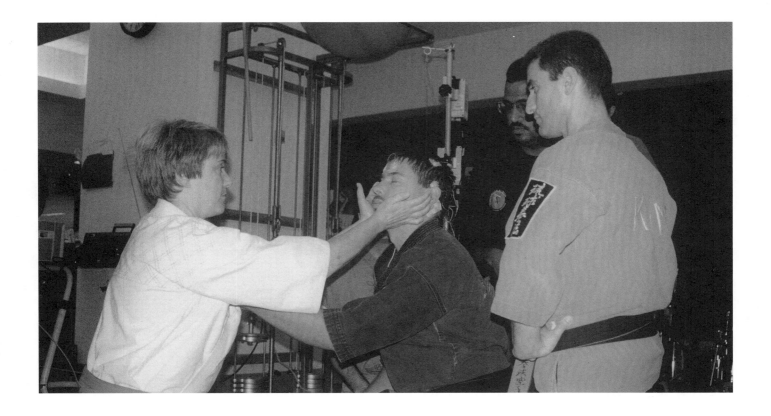

1997 - Kimberly F. Dillman knocks out Bill Burch while kneeling, Mark Kline catches . . . This was part of a medical study at a major university and Burch is wired up to test the results.

A George Dillman knockout to a much larger opponent at the American Karate Studio in Newark, DE.

Ed Parker taught me to make all fighting moves natural, visited my home in Wash., D. C. and worked with my two sons—George, IV and Allen Dillman.

"The Mighty Atom" Joe Greenstein, known for his legendary feats with both mind and body, with George Dillman in the early 1970's. Dillman is a 4 page writeup in the book on Joe Greenstein by Ed Spielman (1979).
Photo by Kim F. Dillman.

GEORGE A. DILLMAN PERFORMANCES!

Madison Square Garden—New York, NY

The Silverdome—Pontiac, MI

Veterans Stadium—Philadelphia, PA

The Spectrum—Philadelphia, PA

JFK Stadium—Washington, D.C.

Baltimore Stadium—Baltimore, MD

West Palm Beach Civic Center—West Palm Beach, FL

Ripley's Believe It or Not Museum—Fisherman's Wharf, San Francisco, CA

Reading Municipal Stadium—Reading, PA

Jackie Gleason Theatre—Miami Beach, FL

Performances were given along with the Dillman Karate Demonstration team, and drew standing ovations from packed-house crowds attending major events.

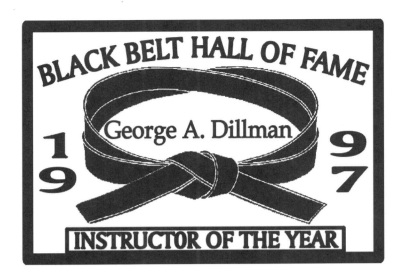

BLACK BELT HALL OF FAME

George A. Dillman

1997

INSTRUCTOR OF THE YEAR

"Pitt-bull" Bob Golden knocks out Brad James 6'7, 280 lb. in front of several hundred people at Christmas self-defense demo.

Will Higginbotham knocks out Mike Curtis with a leg trap and body point.. **Do not do this technique without proper supervision.**

"Pitt-bull" Bob Golden touches out Mark Kramer in front of a full capacity crowd, Dec. 18 1992.

Bill Homann (left), from Valparaiso, IN demonstrates a grab, pull and knockout. His students are Art Chambers, Guz Cruz, Jay Bagley.

Sandra L. Schlessman (left) applies pressure point moves on Greg Dillon at the Dillman Karate International HQ in Reading, PA. Sandra Schlessman, during the late 1970's and early 1980's, was rated by national magazines as the top woman fighter on the East Coast.

Amber Grundhoefer, age 13, KO's dad "Bernie" during a supervised Dillman Theory seminar—Dale, In.

Diane Anderson, Brown Belt, does pressure point knockout on a much larger opponent. Diane is a student of Bob "Pitt Bull" Golden (Dec. 18, 1992). *Photo by Jim Duncan.*

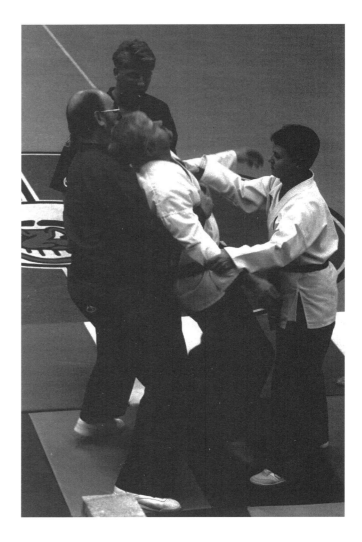

Jim Corn, of Indiana, knocks out a student using a slapping motion from Pinan 4.

Jim Clapp of Newark, DE knocks out a student during advanced belt training at his American Karate Studio.

Following a pressure point takedown, David Wilson of North Vernon, IN puts his opponent in a leg trap and uses points on the foot and back of the head for complete control.

WARNING

This is an educational book,
but these techniques are
NOT TO BE PERFORMED WITHOUT
PROPER SUPERVISION.
We want to share our years of
experience with you, but we do not
want anyone injured.
It is essential that you consult
a physician regarding
whether or not to attempt any
technique shown in this book.
Always have a
Dillman Method instructor
supervise your practice.

Table of Contents

PREFACE

In our earlier book, *KYUSHO-JITSU: The Dillman Method of Pressure Point Fighting*, we presented the fundamental basis of the art of Ryukyu kempo and its distinctive use of pressure points for combat. In this volume we hope to bring the reader to a deeper understanding of the genuine application of traditional martial arts.

This book contains detailed information about the location and use of many of the most important pressure points, as well as introducing the fundamentals of pressure point joint-control techniques. It also includes the performance and breakdown (bunkai) of kata Naihanchi.

Our purpose in presenting these principles is to help you, the reader, to broaden your knowledge and understanding of pressure points and their relationship to the forms of the martial arts. If after reading this book you have a greater appreciation for the movements inherent to your own art, and have gained a deeper insight into the true use of that art, then our efforts will have proven worthwhile.

Bob Golden easily knocks out a much larger opponent during a Chicago area seminar on pressure point fighting.

KATA AND PRESSURE POINTS

Kata can be compared to a song. The meaning of the song is stated in the lyrics and expressed in the melody. If the lyrics are sad, the melody is haunting; if the lyrics are noble, the melody is bold. The meaning of kata is, in its application for real fighting, the expression of that application in the physical movements of the form. But, what if the lyrics are in a foreign language? Without knowing the meaning of the words, how is it possible to truly comprehend the song?

For most students of the martial arts, kata is a song whose lyrics have not been explained. They can appreciate its beauty and power. They have a feel for its rhythms and dynamics. They may even catch some vague sense of its purpose, but without understanding the actual application of the techniques, they cannot truly comprehend the fullness of meaning.

Unfortunately, most karate instructors have not understood the meanings of their own kata, even though they have committed their time and effort to perfecting their performance. Since they can do the kata so well, and since they have found value in their effort, they have decided the question of meaning is not relevant. They have told their students, "This is traditional, don't ask, don't think too much, just do."

However, for the ancient masters of karate, kata was the very essence of combat because they knew not only the outward form but also the application. The kata was alive for these masters because they saw in their minds the exact application of the movements as they performed them. Put together, mental image and physical performance insured that the masters were truly able to fight.

This is why the martial artists of old always insisted that kata alone was sufficient, and that free-sparring was unnecessary. Kata alone was sufficient because these martial artists knew what they were doing and they had no desire to pass on a precious legacy to those who would have no appreciation of what it truly represented. Karate was the ancient Okinawan secret to surviving with strength, dignity, and the ability to defend oneself and one's family in times of foreign occupation.

The Japanese had controlled and militarily occupied Okinawa from 1609. This was the context in which karate developed. The art was practiced and taught in the utmost secrecy due to the threat of reprisals by armed samurai. In fact, the only reason karate went public in 1903 was because of pressure from the Japanese government.

The Japanese had introduced kendo and judo to the Okinawan school curriculum in the hopes of improving the physical condition of potential draftees. Military doctors noticed that some conscripts were in excellent condition. When this was investigated, it was learned that the common element among these young men was that they had trained in Ryukyu kempo (karate). So, effort was made to popularize karate in the school system to improve the quality of the draft-age population.

It is easy to understand how ethnic pride would have encouraged the Okinawans to share some of their art for its health-promoting aspects. But the fact that the Japanese interest in karate was only for fitness purposes would have made karate's masters very reluctant to share the combative secrets of their art. The Okinawans had preserved, treasured and passed on karate in secret — such traditions of secrecy are not easily surrendered. And so, what the Okinawans taught to those school children was a watered down children's art — martial arts for fitness.

After WW II the Americans replaced the Japanese as the occupying political and military presence. How were things any different for the Okinawan martial artists under American occupation, than under Japanese occupation? In many ways things may have seemed worse. The American invasion, like all invasions, had resulted in the deaths of many non-combatants, and naturally the Okinawan populace would be wary of such people. Not only that but, unknowingly, American forces had committed serious cultural crimes. For example, many of the Okinawan mausoleums were destroyed by U.S. personnel who mistook them for military bunkers. Think of how such desecration of tombs would be understood by a people who practice veneration of their ancestors!

Certainly it would be naive to assume that knowledgeable Okinawan masters gladly exchanged their most treasured secrets for a few American dollars, especially when the Americans happily paid cash for far less. Because of the nature of kata, it was a simple matter to teach the outward form of karate, and so, appear to be sharing a great treasure with American students, while withholding the hidden but essential meaning.

Finally, we have recovered that meaning: kata contains the information of kyusho-jitsu, mapping out the location and application, angle and direction for pressure point combat. Yet, we understand that we are still in the process of recovering the application for the particular movements of kata.

And we also realize that the applications we discover for any particular technique may not be what the kata's founder envisioned. But, even where this occurs, the fact that we have real applications, which can truly be used for fighting, which we can visualize as we perform the kata, and which follow the principles of kyusho-jitsu, means that we have at the very least, recaptured the original intention of the kata, if not the exact original application.

In the next chapters we will examine the principles of pressure point fighting. We will also examine the familiar kata Naihanchi shodan, contrasting common (but largely useless) explanations of the kata movements taught among karate styles, with Ryukyu kempo's kyusho-jitsu applications. While the reader will find that this is tremendously revealing, it is of far greater importance that martial artists everywhere develop the skills to look at the forms in their own systems and see the techniques that lie within.

PRINCIPLES OF KATA INTERPRETATION

1. NO "BLOCKS" RULE

Simply put, the movements of kata are not defensive. There are no "downward blocks" or "rising blocks" at all. Blocking is a completely natural action requiring relatively minimal training to attain a good level of skill. But, this is something that every martial artist already knows. In free-sparring blocks occur naturally and without conforming to any particular "technique." What is really needed to learn blocking is a partner to feed the attacks. But, since kata is a solo exercise it is a waste of time to practice blocking the air.

The movements called "blocks" in kata don't work as blocks, anyway. These actions are totally useless — until they are interpreted as offensive actions. Suddenly, a technique that didn't work as a block, works as an attack to pressure points. (This principle is carefully covered in our previous book, *KYUSHO--JITSU: The Dillman Method of Pressure Point Fighting*.)

Now, having taken this position, it is necessary to clarify one important thing: Kyusho-jitsu does contain a defensive element. If an opponent punches, that punch must be addressed. And, the kata movements do indicate how that punch is to be handled. However, what kata shows is definitely not how to block. Rather, it shows which pressure points on the attacking arm or leg are to be struck, touched or grabbed in order to paralyze the limb and/or to set up pressure points on the body or head.

2. PRESSURE POINT RULE

Every kata technique is a pressure point technique. This means that the number one interpretive question on the mind of any student should be, "What pressure points am I using with this movement?" This is not to say that it is impossible to develop some very effective techniques without using kyusho-jitsu principles. But, only pressure point applications can fully and satisfactorily explain the many nuances of kata movements.

There are hundreds of pressure points, each with its own angle and direction for activation. Kata is, quite truthfully, the only way to remember them all. By linking a mental picture of the exact pressure point application with the physical movement of the kata, the mind and body are literally programmed to respond instantly and effectively.

However, it is not necessary to know all the pressure points and to use them in every kata technique. Whatever pressure points a person knows are the pressure points that person should use. While a complete understanding of the Naihanchi kata series, for example, requires familiarity with over 100 acu-points, a meaningful working knowledge of the kata is possible with far fewer.

3. "TWO HAND" RULE

Simply put, there is no wasted or useless part of a kata movement. Every part of the action is there for a reason. There is no "hand at the hip in a ready position." There is no "rear hand moving in the opposite direction to add power to a technique." Both hands in the kata action move because both hands are combative in function. Usually, the rear hand or "withdrawing hand" is grasping the opponent's arm or wrist on pressure points which activate the points that the forward hand is striking.

The majority of kata techniques have a "set position" when one hand is drawn or coiled back, before moving forward. This action is usually interpreted as merely a preparatory movement. But, the truth is, this "preparatory movement" is actually an attack. Many pressure points can only be struck from back to front, and the setting action maps out those points. When the opponent grabs and threatens, he is immediately attacked with the "set position", so that the fight is finished before the first technique is even completed.

Not only do both hands work combatively, but the legs also have an important function. The type of stance used in the execution of a movement affects the direction in which energy is put into the opponent's body. For, example, a horse stance directs energy downward, or to the side; while a front stance beams energy down and forward; and a cross-over stance projects energy beyond the line of the opponent's body.

The legs and feet are also used to step on, rub against, trap or bump pressure points on the opponent's legs. These subtle leg attacks activate points on the body, while also destroying his balance. It is even possible to knock an opponent unconscious using only the action of a basic kata step. The use of the legs in this manner is very advanced, since it requires coordination and sensitivity. Nonetheless, in interpreting a kata movement one should be asking, "What is the purpose of this footwork?"

4. MULTIPLE INTERPRETATION RULE

It is sometimes tempting to ask, what is the meaning of a certain kata move, but the truth is that there are several interpretations. Some say that there should be 100 applications for each technique, others say five. Realistically, one should have at least three. These three are categorized differently by different people. Some say that they should be–release techniques against simple grabs, responses to punches or kicks, defenses against weapon attacks. In our system of Ryukyu kempo, we increase the seriousness of the response, starting with joint manipulation (tuite-waza) to control, moving to more serious knock-out techniques to immobilize, and then finally to killing or crippling applications.

5. DIRECTION OF MOVEMENT RULE

Kata, as everyone knows, moves in a variety of directions. Most students have been told that the direction of movements represents the direction from which various attacks are coming. Nothing could be further from the truth. Kata does not represent fighting against many attackers who come from different directions. Instead, it represents methods of defending against a variety of attacks, which are delivered mostly from the front. The direction of movement in the kata indicates the angle which the defender assumes in relation to the attacker to insure successful application of the technique. For example, a movement to the side means the defender must turn sideways to the attacker while executing the technique; a diagonal step means that the defender must move to the attacker's diagonal to make the technique work 100%.

6. VISUALIZATION RULE

An old piece of wisdom handed down from the masters of old, which never made sense, is this: when performing kata, always visualize the opponent. But, what good did it do to visualize an opponent when the interpretations of the kata movements were so completely useless? With proper understanding of the kata, visualization not only makes sense, it is absolutely essential. Kata is not principally a physical exercise — it is, overall, a mental one. Through the process of visualizing the exact location of pressure points, and properly activating them (including angle and direction) the mind is trained to instantly and accurately respond. The physical actions of the kata close the loop, uniting mind and body, and in the process ingrain real combat skills.

It is also important to work with a partner, practicing the various applications. This allows one to get a tactile sense of how it feels to apply a technique, and this adds to the visualization process. Obviously, working with a partner is a good method of insuring that the applications will really work. **You should have proper supervision, consult a physician, and use restraint.** However, we have found that by visualization alone we are able to develop and use new techniques effectively the first time we try them on someone. The old masters were right when they insisted that kata training — proper and complete kata training— was all that was necessary.

Jack Hogan (Jacksonville, FL) demonstrates very advanced pressure point fighting by knocking out two opponents at the same time during a local TV show.

PRINCIPLES OF KYUSHO-JITSU

Since oriental martial arts are inseparably bound to oriental culture, it is to be expected that the arts would conform, both superficially and substantively with the Asian world view. Arts with strong roots in Taoist thinking (tai chi, hsing-i, etc.) are characterized by the concepts of yin and yang, the five elements and so on. Among arts of Buddhist origin (e.g. shaolin-chuan) we find Buddhist concepts and elements. In the same way, it is to be expected that kyusho-jitsu, or pressure point combat, would be based on Eastern concepts. If this art had developed in the West we would expect nerve plexii and baro-receptors, motor-nerve points and neural pathways to be the descriptive language employed. Since this is an Asian art, and the primary medical practice in that part of the world is acupuncture, we find, as expected, that acupuncture terminology and concepts form the theoretical basis for kyusho-jitsu.

Traditional Chinese medicine, unlike modern Western medicine, is based on clinical observation, rather than controlled experimentation. The Chinese carefully observed the results of certain actions, but did not experiment to determine the mechanisms at work. Instead, they formed theories about what was happening using concepts from their philosophical cosmology — a cosmology based on a unity (the One, or the Tao) which becomes the duality (yin and yang), which in turn generates the five fundamental elements (earth, metal, water, wood, fire).

This means that the explanation for a given effect of acupuncture or kyusho-jitsu may or may not be scientifically accurate. There may be no concrete reality which corresponds to the acupuncture interpretations. For example, acupuncture anesthesia in the past may have been explained as energy flow and the inter-action of the five elements. Now the anesthesia effect is commonly explained as being due the release of endogenous morphine (endorphines) in the brain as a result of needling.

However, from our perspective as martial artists, what is important is the effect which we achieve. We are interested in results, even if we cannot accurately explain the mechanisms which produce those results. In our search for deeper interpretations and applications of our kata, it is not so important whether "fire" actually melts "metal" (see p. 56). What is important is that this general framework can predict what will happen when we perform some particular technique, and can guide us in successfully discovering deeper meanings for kata techniques.

By using the language and principles of acupuncture as the theoretical basis for our study, we are better able to understand what the founders of karate intended in their kata. It isn't important for our purposes if the acupuncture explanation for an event is scientifically correct, so long as the principle works. And our experience shows that it does work.

In order to perform a kyusho-jitsu technique it is only necessary to know the proper point combination and the proper angle and direction. After adequate practice of kata (with visualization) and bunkai these techniques can successfully be applied. However, to be better able to analyze kata in order to gain deeper insights into the art and develop additional pressure point techniques, one should become familiar with the general principles of oriental medicine (acupuncture) and how those principles relate to combat.

The Eastern viewpoint is a holistic one. The body is understood as a wholly interactive, interrelated, and integrated organism. The health of each part of the body depends on the wellness of the whole. In fact, health is defined as the proper balance of intrinsic energy, or life force.

This energy, called ki, flows through the body along pathways or channels called meridians. Along the meridians are discreet points which serve as gateways or valves by which the flow of energy can be controlled. These points are known as tsubo (a shiatsu term which roughly means "pressure point") or kyusho (which roughly means "vulnerable point" or "vital point").

The healer manipulates these points with fingertip pressure (shiatsu) or needles (acupuncture) in an effort to restore and maintain a proper balance of energy in the body. The kyusho-jitsu exponent attacks these points in order to disrupt the balance of energy.

There are 361 "regular" points which are scattered across 14 meridian channels. There are also some 391 "extraordinary" points which have been identified, but which are not as widely used in medicine. The meridians upon which the points are found are related to the various organs of the body. These associations are determined through the clinical observation that stimulating the points on a particular meridian had a noticeable effect on the corresponding organ.

Meridians are also classified in two other ways. In oriental thinking there are two polar opposites which together make-up all things. These are the yin and the yang, the negative and positive, the spiritual and substantial, the female and male. Each channel is either yin or yang, according to its energy flow. Also, in oriental philosophy there are five elements which describe the physical characteristics of all things. These elements are earth, metal, water, wood, and fire, and each meridian is characterized by one of these elements.

Therefore, to understand kyusho-jitsu one should be generally familiar with the meridians and know four important features of each: 1. To what organ does it relate? 2. What is its energy, yin or yang? 3. What element characterizes it? 4. Where is each meridian located?

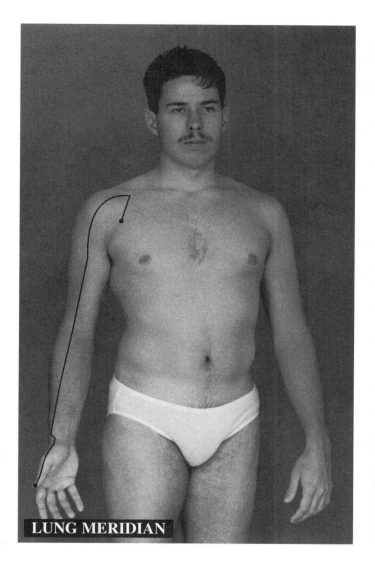

LUNG MERIDIAN

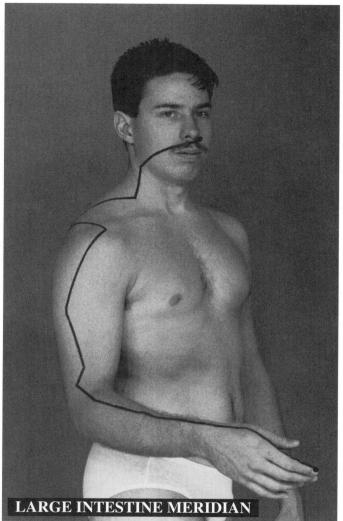

LARGE INTESTINE MERIDIAN

LUNG MERIDIAN

The lung meridian begins at the upper corner of the chest and proceeds down the inner aspect of the arm on the thumb side, ending in the tip of the thumb. It is a yin meridian with 11 points. Its element is metal.

LARGE INTESTINE MERIDIAN

The large intestine meridian begins at the tip of the index finger and travels up the outer aspect of the arm on the thumb side, across the shoulders and the neck to end at the corner of the nose. It is a yang meridian with 20 points. Its element is metal.

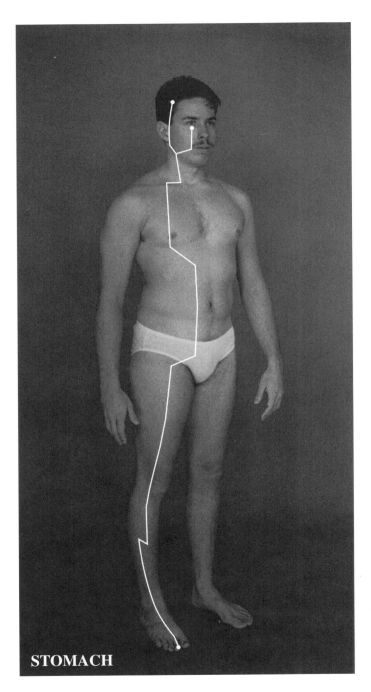

STOMACH

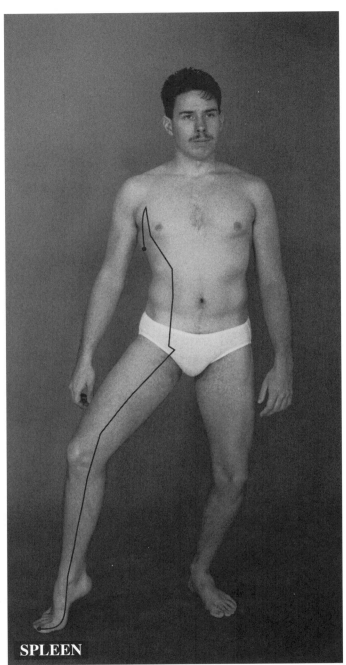

SPLEEN

STOMACH MERIDIAN

The stomach meridian begins directly under the eye and proceeds down the neck, torso and the leg to end at the tip of the second toe. It is a yang meridian with 45 points. Its element is earth.

SPLEEN MERIDIAN

The spleen meridian originates at the tip of the big toe and moves upward along the inside of the leg and up to the torso to end at the side of the body. It is a yin meridian with 21 points, and its element is earth.

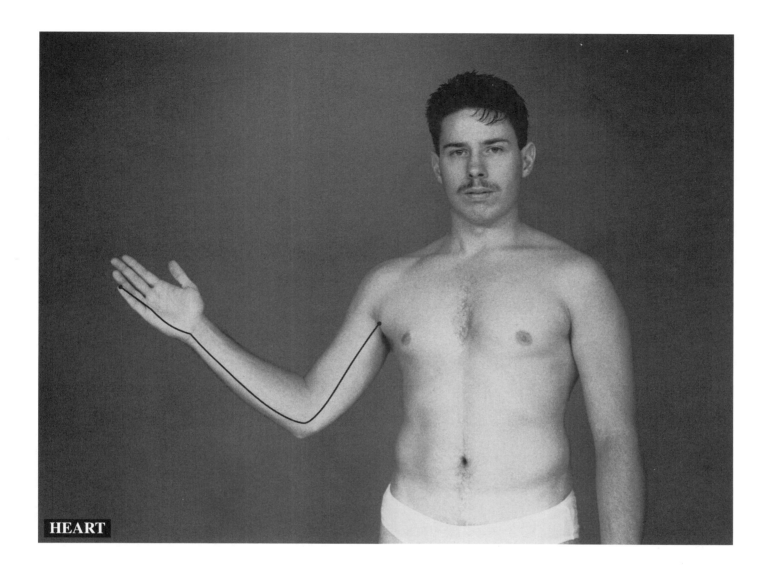

HEART

HEART MERIDIAN

The heart meridian starts in the armpit and travels down the inside of the arm on the little finger side, terminating at the tip of the little finger. It is a yin meridian with 9 points, and its element is fire.

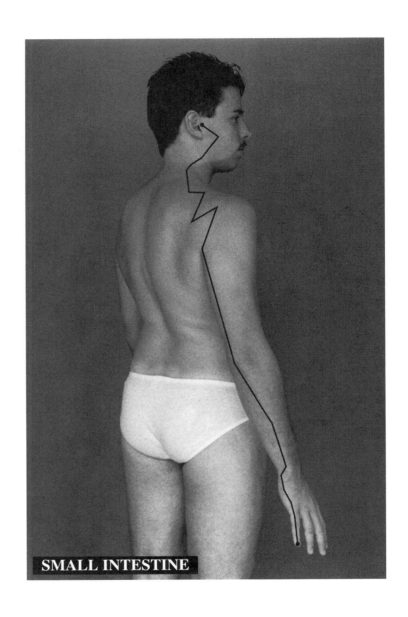

SMALL INTESTINE

SMALL INTESTINE MERIDIAN

The small intestine meridian begins at the tip of the little finger and runs up the outer aspect of the arm on the little finger side, across the shoulder and onto the side of the head, where it ends at the ear. It is a yang meridian, having 19 points, and its element is fire.

BLADDER MERIDIAN

The bladder meridian originates at the inner corner of the eye, moves up over the head, then down the back in two lines running parallel to the spine. It then follows down the back of the leg and terminates at the little toe. It is a yang meridian with 67 points, and its element is water.

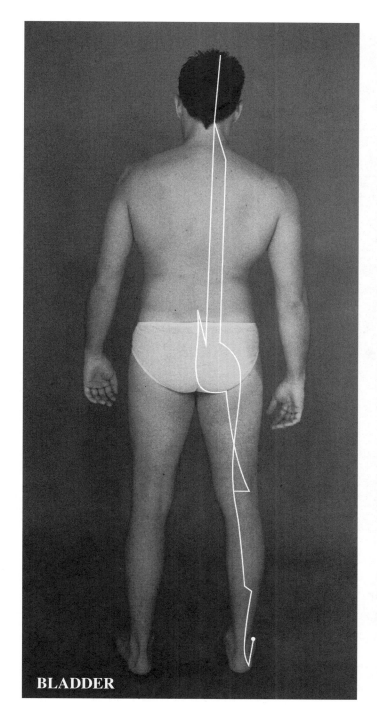

BLADDER

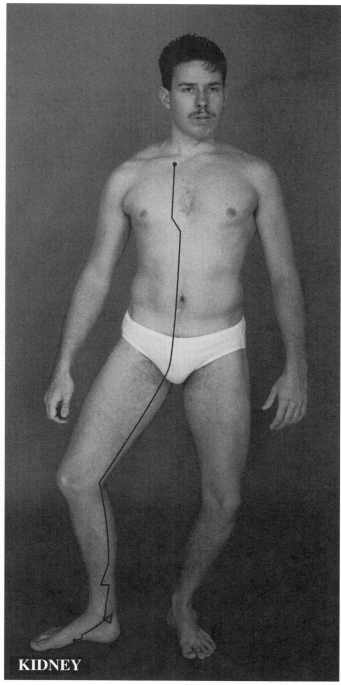

KIDNEY

KIDNEY MERIDIAN

    The kidney meridian begins in the sole of the foot, and travels up the inside of the leg, past the genitals and up the torso just beside the mid-line, to terminate just below the collar bone. It is a yin meridian with 27 points and its element is water.

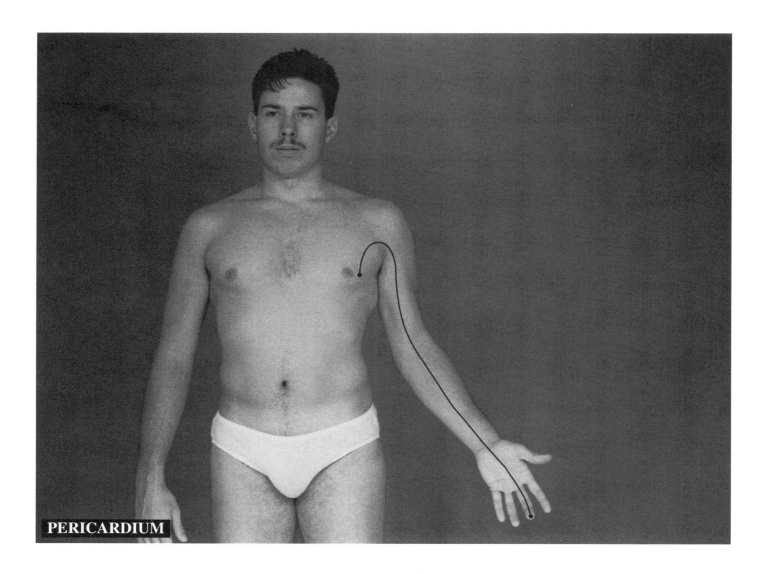

PERICARDIUM

PERICARDIUM MERIDIAN

The pericardium meridian begins on the chest, near the nipple, from there it flows up to the shoulder, then down the middle of the arm to end at the tip of the middle finger. It is a yin meridian with 9 points. Its element is fire.

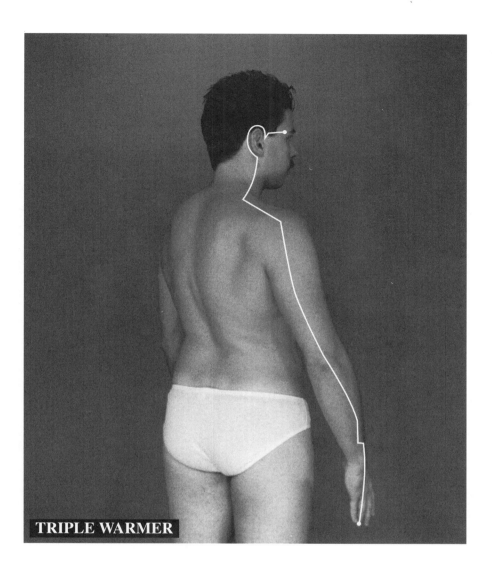

TRIPLE WARMER

TRIPLE WARMER MERIDIAN

The triple warmer meridian originates at the tip of the ring (fourth) finger, and follows the back of the arm along the mid-line, up to the shoulder. It continues across the back surface of the shoulder, then onto the head, where it flows around the border of the ear to end at the temple. It is a yang meridian with 23 points, and its element is fire.

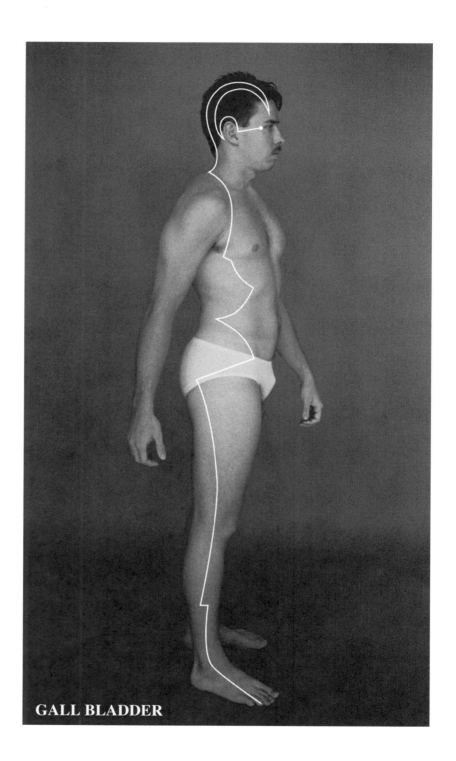

GALL BLADDER

GALL BLADDER MERIDIAN

The gall bladder meridian begins at the outer corner of the eye, then follows a zig-zag route around the ear, back to the forehead, across the top of the head and down the rear side of the neck. From there it travels down the side of the body to end at the tip of the fourth toe. It is a yang meridian with 44 points and its element is wood.

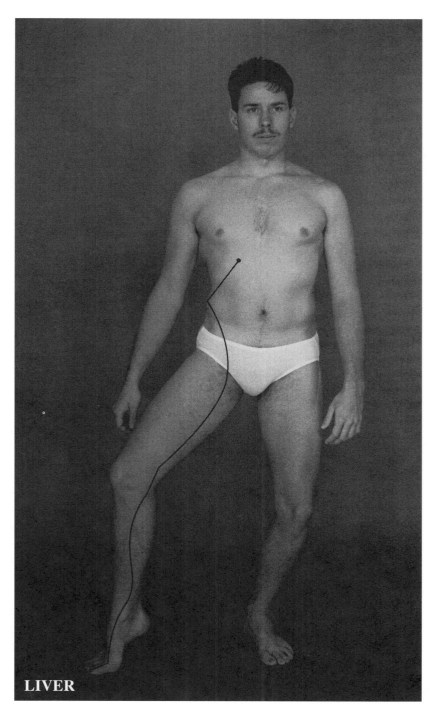

LIVER

LIVER MERIDIAN
The liver meridian begins at the tip of the big toe, and follows upward along the inside of the leg, and onto the abdomen to terminate at the border of the rib cage. It is a yin meridian with 14 points. Its element is wood.

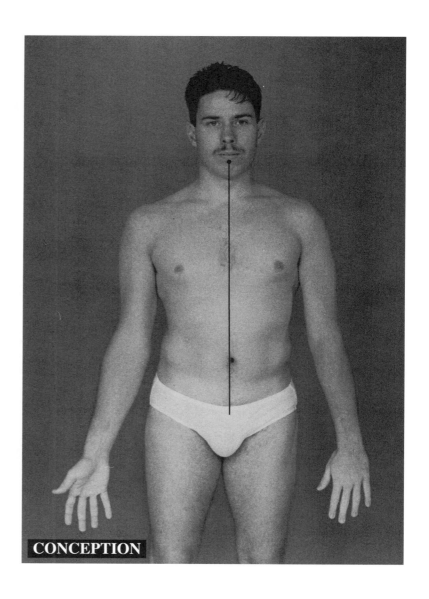

CONCEPTION

CONCEPTION MERIDIAN

The two centerline meridians (conception and governor) are not related to any specific organ, but are important in the regulation of ki. The conception meridian begins in the crotch, midway between the anus and the scrotum on men, and midway between the anus and the commisura labiorum on women. It travels up the front of the body, along the centerline to end just below the lower lip. This meridian is the primary source line of yin-ki (yin energy) and all yin-meridians are related to it. The conception channel has 24 points.

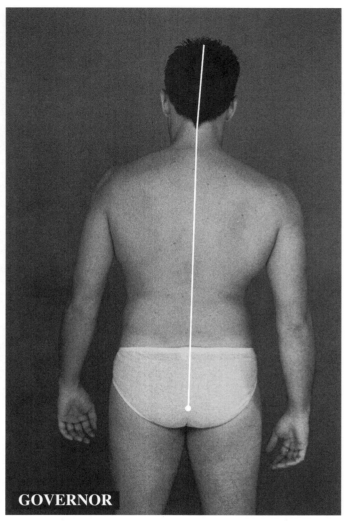

GOVERNOR MERIDIAN

The governor meridian begins at the tip of tail-bone and travels upward along the spine, over the head to terminate inside the top lip. This meridian is the "governor" of yang-ki (yang energy) and all yang meridians are related to it. The governor channel has 28 points.

CAUTION:
The examples given to illustrate the principles in the following section are serious kyusho-jitsu techniques. Remember to seek instruction under a qualified teacher before attempting pressure point methods.

ACUPUNCTURE PRINCIPLES OF KYUSHO-JITSU

There are five rules of kyusho-jitsu which are based on the principles of acupuncture: 1) Attack along the meridian; 2) Attack yin and yang; 3) Attack in accordance with the diurnal cycle; 4) Attack in the cycle of destruction; 5) The special points.

ATTACK ALONG THE MERIDIAN

One of the most basic methods of kyusho-jitsu is to successively attack points along any particular meridian. Typically, this will begin with points on the extremities, then move along the channel to finish at points on the body or the head. Often, the last point attacked is the first or last point on the meridian.

For example, grasp an opponent's left wrist with your left hand, on wrist points L-8 and (particularly) H-6. Then forcefully strike the inside of his arm, just above the elbow at H-2 with the thumb of your right fist. Your opponent's left arm will involuntarily swing away from his body, and he will lean towards you. This will expose H-1, the first point for the heart meridian, located in the armpit, which you punch with the tip of the knuckle of the thumb. [A-F]

NOTE: Remember to always seek out proper instruction and supervision before attempting to study and learn pressure points, and always use the utmost restraint in practice. We strongly recommend that the reader refrain from actually striking H-1, since even a moderate blow can cause the arm to go numb.

Warning: Do not strike heart points because you do not know the condition of your opponent's heart.

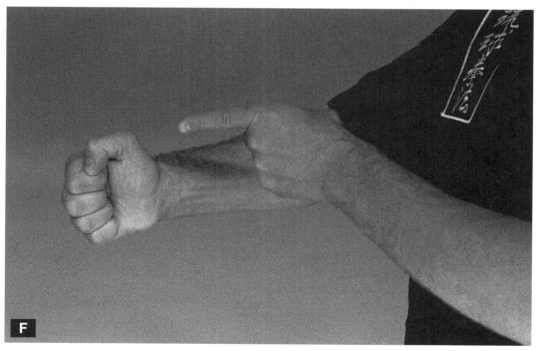

ATTACK YIN AND YANG

As already explained, each meridian is either yin or yang, depending on the direction of the energy flow. Since yin and yang are intended to coexist in balance and harmony, it is clear that each yin must have a balancing yang. In acupuncture this balance of yin and yang is quite specific. Of the twelve bi-lateral visceral (organ-related) channels, six are yin and six are yang. And these channels are arranged into six circuits (on each side of the body). The characteristic of these circuits is that one meridian is yin, the other yang, and both meridians are the same element.

The circuits might be compared to electrical wiring. There is a positive and a negative wire and both are needed for the electric current to flow. For example energy flows down the inside of the arm to the tip of the little finger in the heart channel, then it flows up from the little finger on the outside of the arm along the small intestine meridian. These circuits are known in healing as the feng-shu relationship.

The meridians are related as follows:

YIN ORGANS	YANG ORGANS
Lung —	Large Intestine
Spleen —	Stomach
Heart —	Small Intestine
Kidney —	Bladder
Pericardium —	Triple Warmer
Liver —	Gall Bladder

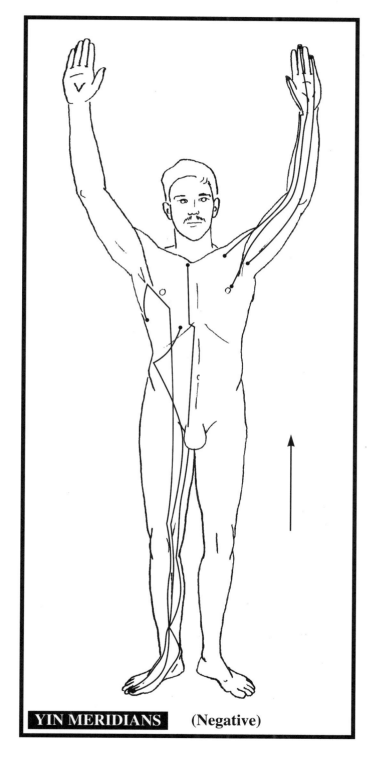

YIN MERIDIANS (Negative)

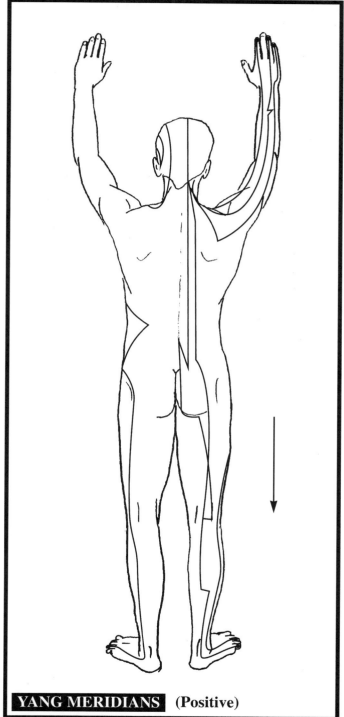

YANG MERIDIANS (Positive)

In kyusho-jitsu, this circuit can be used in ways similar to the rule of the meridians. Rather than striking along one single meridian, it is possible to use two meridians in a circuit. Striking along the lung channel effects the large intestine line, and vice-versa. For example, a joint lock against the index finger affects the large intestine (yang) meridian. The lung is the corresponding yin organ. Therefore, while locking the index finger, attack with a punch to L-1, the first point on the lung channel. [A]

Attacking yin and yang can also be understood in a more general manner. The front of the body can be designated as yin, the back as yang. The left side is yin, the right yang. The top half is yin, the bottom half is yang. This means that pressure point techniques which cross the body — front to back, side to side, top to bottom, or diagonally, as in right upper back to left lower front — are applying the yin/yang principle.

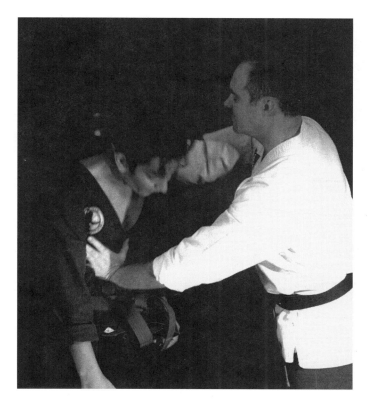

Top left: Damon Davidson of Hixon, Tennesse, knocks out Seros Farajian.

Top right: They do this in Texas... Randy Fuller uses Nai Hanchi kata move to tap out Charlie Dean of Silsbee, Texas.

Bottom: Mark Kline, of Piscataway, NJ, knocks out Marc Pollack using a body-crossing attack to gall bladder points.

ATTACK IN ACCORDANCE WITH THE DIURNAL CYCLE

As ki flows through the body it follows a twenty four hour (diurnal) cycle through all twelve of the visceral meridians. The succession of ki flow is as follows:

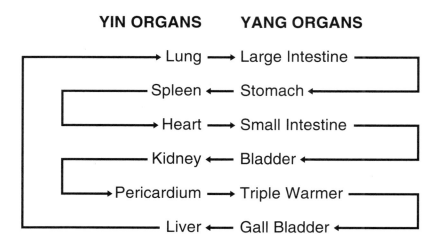

This has two implications for kyusho-jitsu: point sequence and time of day attacking.

The lung and the large intestine form a yin/yang circuit. The daily flow of ki, moves from lung, to large intestine, then to stomach. This means that it is possible to move from large intestine to either lung (yin/yang) or stomach (diurnal cycle) when performing techniques.

For example, when an opponent grabs your lapels, a strike against LI-10 will bring his head forward in such a manner that the point S-5 along the jaw becomes vulnerable. This occurs in accord with the twenty four hour cycle. [A-D]

In very advanced kyusho-jitsu, this principle is used exactly. Each meridian is particularly vulnerable for two hours in twenty four. By attacking a meridian during its active time, techniques have a magnified effect.

But by attacking a particular meridian during its weakest stage of activity it is possible to create a result which won't be felt until the meridian enters its strong period twelve hours later. This is a form of delayed pressure point fighting.

ATTACK IN THE CYCLE OF DESTRUCTION

The twelve bi-lateral meridians are each assigned one of five elements. In the Chinese cosmology, each element is responsible for generating another element to form a complete cycle. Likewise, each element destroys another element in cycle. This principle has been used by acupuncturists for centuries. If, for example, the problem exists along the lung meridian, the acupuncturist might stimulate the stomach or spleen meridian, because "earth" stimulates and benefits "metal." likewise, if a problem manifests itself on the lung meridian, the acupuncturist may diagnose a problem on the heart meridian, since heart is "fire", which destroys "metal".

CYCLE OF CREATION **CYCLE OF DESTRUCTION**

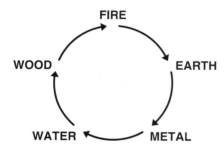 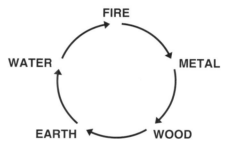

A method for remembering the cycle of creation is to state it in these terms: FIRE generates EARTH (think of the dirty ashes of a camp fire); EARTH generates METAL (visualize iron "clinkers" found in the cold ashes of a fire); METAL generates WATER (think of condensation on a metal container); WATER generates WOOD (visualize rain in a forest, or sap dripping from a tree); WOOD generates FIRE (think of burning logs in a camp fire).

A good device for remembering the cycle of destruction is to remember it in this fashion: FIRE melts METAL; METAL cuts WOOD; WOOD (as in a tree's roots) penetrates the EARTH; EARTH (as in the bank of a river, or an earthen dam) obstructs WATER; and WATER quenches FIRE.

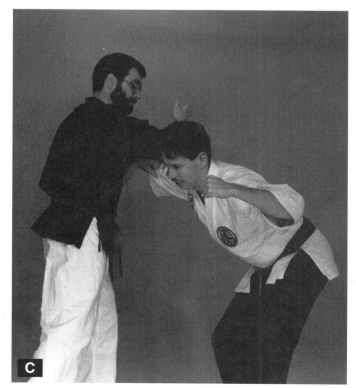

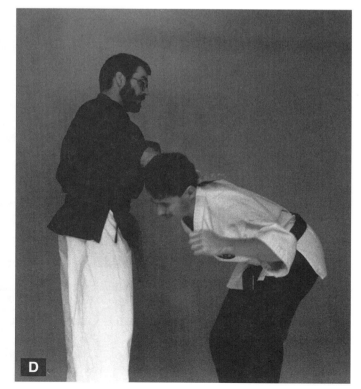

(Note: explanation, next page)

For purposes of combat, follow the cycle of destruction. For example, a strike to the inguinal crease point cluster (see Chapter Three on pressure points for exact location) strikes two points, Sp-12 and Li-12. Spleen has the elemental value earth and liver has the elemental value wood. Wood penetrates earth, this is one step in the cycle of destruction. As a result of striking this target, the opponent will double over, but his face will remain upright. Exactly at the bend of his neck is the point B-10. Bladder has the elemental value water, and earth obstructs water. By striking B-10, a second step in the cycle of destruction is achieved, and the opponent is knocked unconscious. **(CAUTION: This is a serious technique which should not actually be performed but only indicated in practice.)** [A-D] There are certain places in kata which sequentially attack points through one complete cycle of destruction. These techniques are considered lethal.

THE SPECIAL POINTS

In addition to these rules for pressure point fighting, the serious practitioner also needs to understand the special points. There are two main sets of special points these are called mu, or "alarm" points and shu, or "associated" points. Alarm points lie (mostly) on the front of the torso. There is an alarm point for each of the twelve organs. They are used diagnostically because they become tender when there is a problem with the corresponding organ.

The associated points are all found on the back, along the Bladder meridian. Like the alarm points, there is an associated point for each organ. In kyusho-jitsu, the alarm and associated points function in conjunction with the related meridians.

There are other special purpose points, and in the chapter on pressure points, we will mention some of these. In particular are the intersection points (places where meridians "communicate" with each other) which are useful in yin and yang strikes.

The task in kata interpretation is determining what combination of points to use to create an effective application for each technique. The four acupuncture based rules of kyusho-jitsu are important keys to unlocking kata's hidden secrets. In analyzing kata, the initial action of the movement will often suggest a particular point as a starting place. The subsequent action can then be interpreted using the four rules. Ask, "Does the continuation of the kata movement seem to attack again on the same meridian? Does it indicate an attack to the corresponding yin or yang meridian? Does it seem to follow the 24 hour cycle? Does it fit the cycle of destruction?" Additionally, one should watch for the use of any special points.

Also, bear in mind that a technique may touch several principles at once. Attacking lung then large intestine combines yin and yang with the diurnal cycle, since the ki flows from lung [yin] to large intestine [yang].

Experience shows that, not only are kata organized in a manner consistent with these principles, but, in application, the reactions of the opponent's body actually fit the kata movements. Time and time again we find that striking one point will automatically expose one or more follow-up points in accordance with one or more of these concepts.

MERIDIAN	ALARM POINT	ASSOCIATED POINT
LUNG	L-1	B-13
LARGE INTESTINE	S-25	B-25
STOMACH	Co-12	B-21
SPLEEN	Li-13	B-20
HEART	Co-14	B-15
SMALL INTESTINE	Co-4	B-27
BLADDER	Co-3	B-28
KIDNEY	GB-25	B-23
PERICARDIUM	Co-17	B-14
TRIPLE WARMER	Co-5	B-22
GALL BLADDER	GB-24	B-19
LIVER	Li-14	B-18

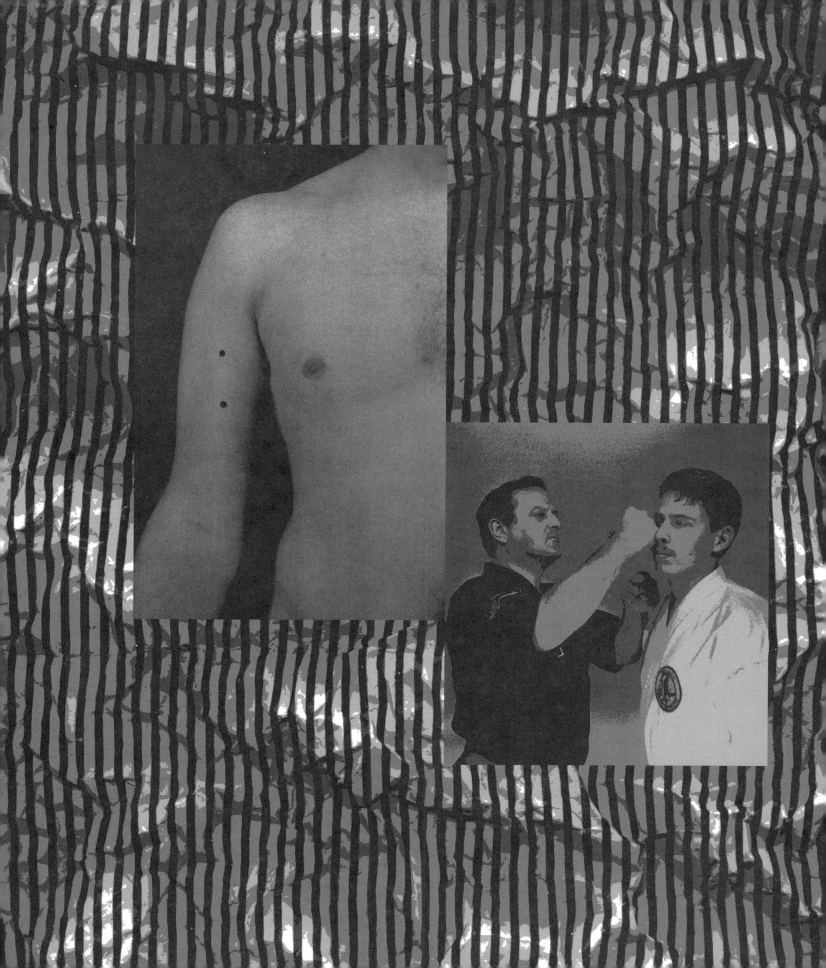

THE PRESSURE POINTS

Because of the obvious danger of simply playing around with pressure points, the following rules of training must be strictly observed.

1. Train only under a qualified instructor.

2. Do not work on pressure points for more than fifteen minutes per week.

3. When training, do not switch sides. Only strike on one side of the body in any given training session.

4. Do not apply cross-body techniques, that is: do not strike corresponding points on opposite sides of your partner's body.

5. Be sure to learn proper revival techniques (See *Kyusho-jitsu: The Dillman Method of Pressure Point Fighting*, chapter five, or Dillman Video #5).

6. Do not work pressure points on persons with health problems, or people over the age of 40, or people on drugs (legal or otherwise).

7. Use the utmost restraint at all times. It is not necessary to knock someone out cold to see the effect of a pressure point. Usually a light blow is sufficient to demonstrate effectiveness.

Since the first rule of kata interpretation is that every action is applied against pressure points, then familiarity with pressure points is essential for truly understanding the kata. In our first book, we presented the location of several pressure points and important information concerning them. The reader is urged to be thoroughly familiar with that material before attempting to master the contents of this text.

Common acupuncture nomenclature is being used to designate various pressure points. This is to assist the reader to research further by referring to texts on acupuncture. In a few cases so-called "extraordinary" points — those not lying on the 14 classically identified regular meridians — are mentioned. Because these points are only found in the most complete acupuncture texts, they are mentioned in connection with common points. In this way, the reader will have an appropriate reference.

It also needs to be mentioned that the English translations of the various channel names are not always consistent from text to text. In particular, the triple warmer is variously identified as the triple burner, three metabolisms, three fires, thyroid, or sanjiao channel. And the pericardium is often called the governor of the heart.

In describing these points, the designation AU will often appear. AU stands for anatomical unit. This is what is sometimes called a "body inch" or cun in Chinese. The AU is different for every person, but the average length 1 AU = 1/2 - 1 inch. One AU is equal to the width of the thumb at the middle joint. [DIAGRAM]

The best process for locating points is to begin by locating them on oneself using AU measurements and finger-tip pressure. Generally, you will be able to feel when you are on a point. Once you are familiar with the location of points on your own body, practice locating them on the bodies of various training partners. Do not underestimate the importance of this step: accuracy is everything in kyusho-jitsu.

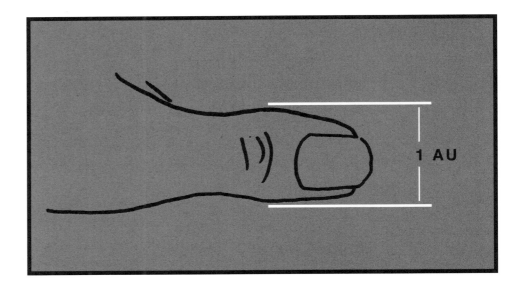

POINT CLUSTERS

A casual glance at an acupuncture chart can give the impression that there are countless places on the body where several points can be struck with one hand. However, this is somewhat misleading. In certain places, such as the wrist at H-6, there are several points in very close proximity. The chart will show that in the space of just 1.5 AU, there are four points: H-4 through H-7. In kyusho-jitsu, different from acupuncture, these points do not function as separate. They possess overlapping areas of activation, and operate (for combative purposes) as a single point.

Other places have points in close proximity without overlapping areas of activation, which, it would appear, could be struck with a single blow. For example, there are three points in a row on the side of the neck, S-9, LI-18 and SI-16. Clearly a palm up knife-hand strike could hit all three points simultaneously. However, these points must each be struck from a different angle and direction. S-9 is hit diagonally front to back, LI-18 from the side and SI-16 diagonally from back to front. This means that even if a blow lands on all three points, only one will be activated depending on the angle of impact.

There are certain places on the body where two or more points exist in a group having the following characteristics: 1. The points do not have overlapping areas of activation; 2. The points respond to the same type of method (rub, touch, strike, knead); 3. The points have the same angle and direction of activation; 4. The points can be reached with one hand (or foot). In the course of describing pressure points, we will describe these point clusters and their use.

Points of the hand & arm

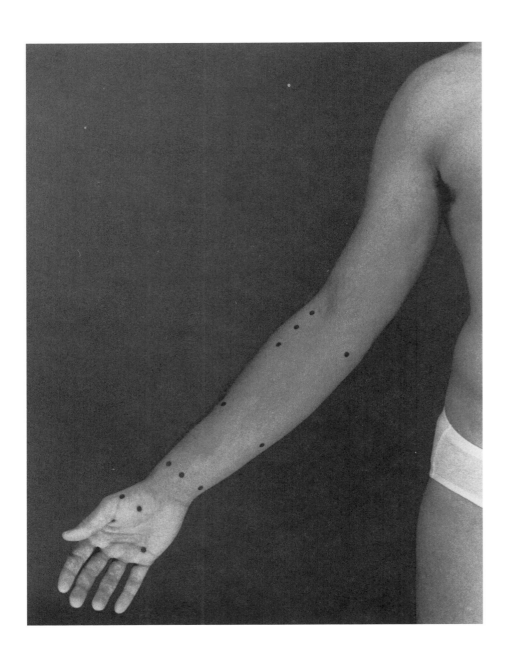

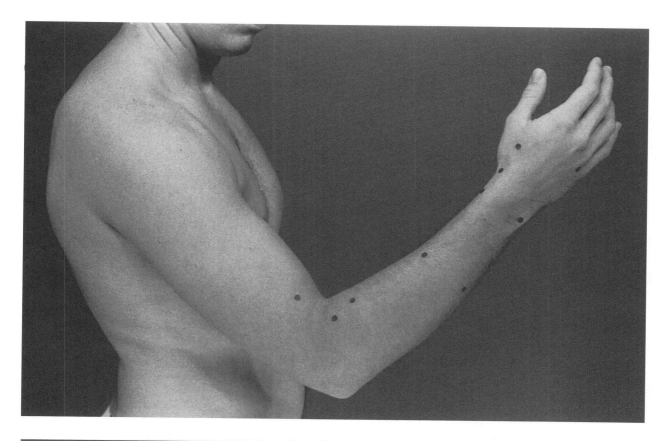

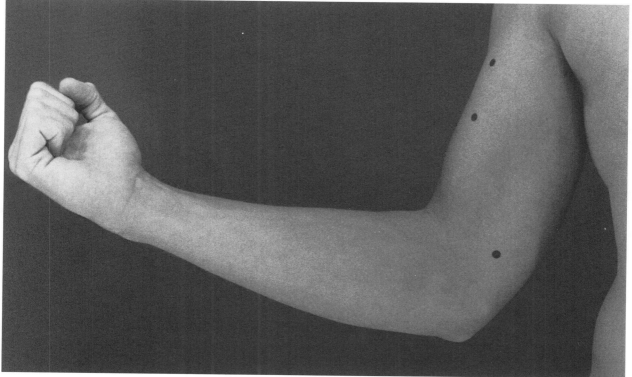

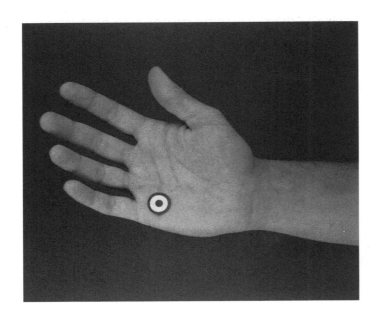

HEART # 8: H-8

LOCATION: On the palm of the hand between the 4th and 5th metacarpals, in the fourth lumbrical muscle and the tendon of the digitorum sublimis muscle. When the hand is closed into a (loose) fist, the tip of the little finger rests on this point.

ANATOMY: The common palmar digital artery and vein, and the fourth common palmar digital branch of the ulnar nerve.

METHOD: Press with the tips of the fingers into this point when executing tuite maneuvers which torque against the little finger. Typically this point is used in conjunction with LI-4 or LI-5. [A, B]

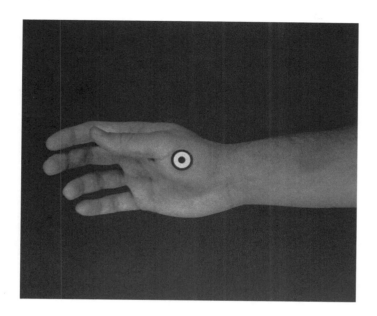

LUNG # 10: L-10

LOCATION: Located at about the mid-point of the first metacarpal, on the thenar prominence in the lateral abductor pollicis brevis and opponens pollicis muscles. It is found in the "meat of the thumb" on the borderline between the (reddish) skin of the palm and the skin of the back of the hand.

ANATOMY: A branch of the cephalic vein of the thumb, the lateral cutaneous nerve of the forearm and a superficial branch of the radial nerve.

METHOD: press with the fingertips against the bone of the thumb. This point is used when squeezing the thumb towards the little finger in tuite techniques. [A]

M-UE-13:

LOCATION: This is an "extraordinary point" located one AU lateral to L-10 more deeply into the "meat of the thumb".

ANATOMY: A branch of the cephalic vein of the thumb, the lateral cutaneous nerve of the forearm and a superficial branch of the radial nerve.

METHOD: Press the fingertips into this point to execute wrist turning tuite techniques, usually used in conjunction with TW-3 on the back of the hand.

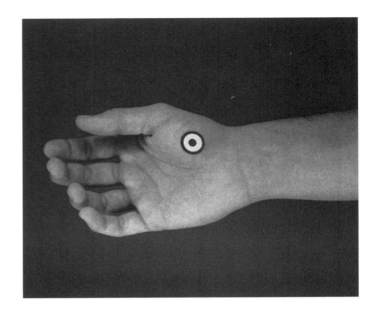

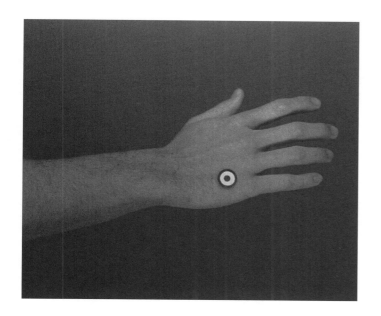

TRIPLE WARMER # 3: TW-3

LOCATION: 1 AU proximal to the metacarpalphalangeal joints (knuckles) between the 4th and 5th metacarpals on the dorsal aspect of the hand in the fourth interosseous muscle. It is on the back of the hand, about one third of the distance from the knuckles to the wrist, between the bones of the fourth and fifth fingers.

ANATOMY: A dorsal branch of the ulnar nerve.

METHOD: Press this point with the thumb when executing wrist reversal methods of tuite, usually with M-UE-13 (above). It may also be struck to immobilize the hand. [A, B]

LARGE INTESTINE # 4: LI-4

LOCATION: In the dorsal interosseus muscle between the 1st and 2nd metacarpals. It is in the "web of the thumb" slightly towards the bone of the index finger.

ANATOMY: A superficial branch of the radial nerve.

METHOD: Press this point firmly against the side of the index finger bone (2nd metacarpal), when performing tuite techniques. [A] Typically, it is used in conjunction with SI-6.

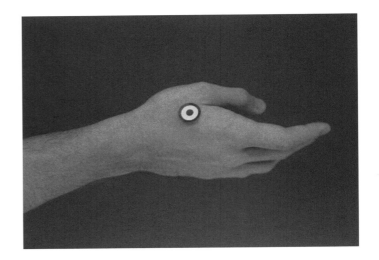

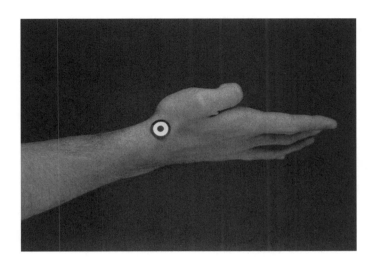

LARGE INTESTINE # 5: LI-5

LOCATION: In the hollow between the extensor pollicis longus and the extensor pollicis brevis. It is found in the depression between the two tendons at the base of the thumb.

ANATOMY: A superficial branch of the radial nerve.

METHOD: Press with the tip of the thumb between the tendons and towards the wrist. [A] This point also responds well to a strike, but it is difficult to hit.

SMALL INTESTINE # 6: SI-6,

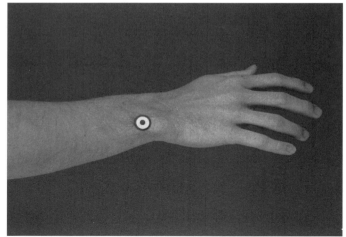

LOCATION: 1/2 AU up (proximal) from the crease of the wrist on the back (dorsal aspect) of the forearm, in the cleft of the bony nob (styloid process) of the ulna.

ANATOMY: The dorsal branch of the ulnar nerve, and branches of the posterior antebrachial cutaneous nerve.

METHOD: Press this point against the bone and towards the hand to bend the wrist. Alternately, press this point and LI-4 (Page 70) towards each other in tuite-waza. [A-C]

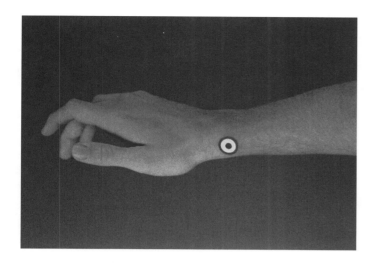

LUNG # 7: L-7

LOCATION: 1.5 AU from the crease of the wrist, in the depression just behind the bony prominence (styloid process) of the radius, on the thumb side of the forearm.

ANATOMY: The lateral antebrachial cutaneous nerve, the superficial ramus of the radial nerve, and the cephalic vein.

METHOD: This point may be pressed, or rubbed towards the wrist to weaken the hand. When grabbing the wrist, roll the thumb across L-7, while squeezing against SI-6 (above) with the fingertips. [A, B]

NOTE: The side of the wrist is an excellent variation on the ridgehand strike. However, when using this method, it is important to turn the wrist slightly outward to avoid hitting your L-7 point against the opponent's body, thus weakening your own hand. [C]

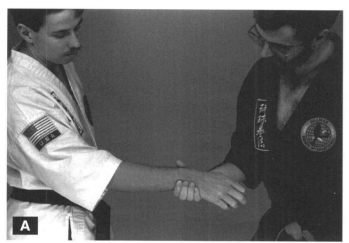

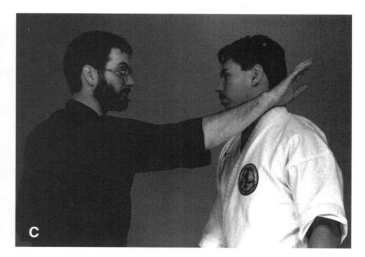

HEART # 6: H-6

LOCATION: 1/2 AU up (proximal) from the crease of the wrist, on the inside (palmar aspect) of the forearm, against the ulnar bone and next to the tendon of the flexor carpi ulnaris.
ANATOMY: The ulnar nerve, and the medial antebrachial cutaneous nerve
METHOD: Push this point against the ulnar bone and towards the hand to weaken the grip and the wrist. [A]

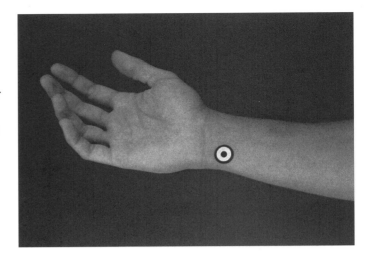

LUNG # 8: L-8

LOCATION: One AU up (proximal) from the crease of the wrist in the depression by the radial artery (about the place a nurse takes a pulse).
ANATOMY: The lateral antebrachial cutaneous nerve, the superficial ramus of the radial nerve.
METHOD: Press into the depression next to the radial bone, and up towards the wrist to weaken the hand. When grasping the wrist from the outside, squeeze the fingertips into this point, while pressing the thumb into H-6 (above). [A]

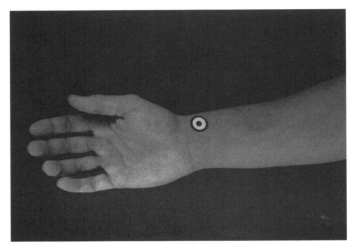

A

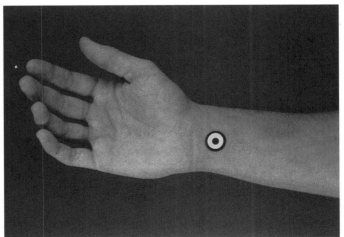

PERICARDIUM # 6: P-6

LOCATION: Between the tendons of the flexor carpi radialis and the flexor digitorum sublimis muscle two AU above (proximal) from the center of the transverse crease in the wrist. This point can be found in the soft space between the tendons of the wrist.
ANATOMY: The medial and lateral cutaneous nerves of the forearm. This point lies directly on the medial nerve.
METHOD: Press in and towards the fist to weaken the hand. When grabbing the wrist, this point can be substituted for H-6, since the pericardium and heart meridians are both yin meridians of the element fire. [A]

A

LUNG # 6: L-6

LOCATION: On the radial aspect of the forearm, 6 AU up (proximal) from the crease of the wrist, in the brachioradialis muscle, at the upper extremity of the pronator teres muscle and the medial margin of the extensor carpi radialis brevis and longus muscles. This point can be found on the thumb-side of the arm about halfway between the wrist and the elbow.

ANATOMY: The lateral cutaneous nerve of the forearm and a superficial branch of the radial nerve.

METHOD: Strike this point towards the fist to weaken the fist. [A]

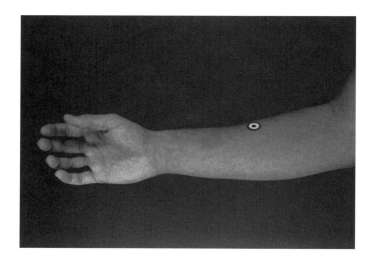

M-UE-28

LOCATION: In the flexor carpi ulnaris and the flexor digitorum profundus, 5 AU up (proximal) from the wrist, on the little finger side of the forearm.

ANATOMY: The ulnar nerve and the palmar cutaneous branch of that nerve.

METHOD: Strike this point upwards against the ulnar bone to weaken the wrist.

NOTE: This is an excellent point to use when disarming an opponent.

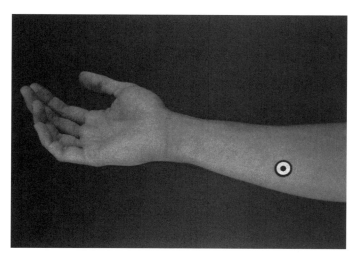

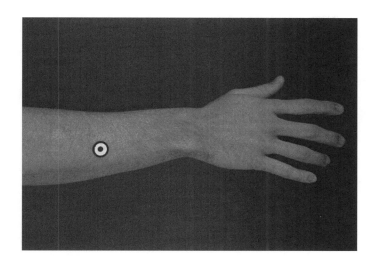

SMALL INTESTINE # 7: SI-7

LOCATION: In the middle of the forearm, 5 AU up (proximal) from the wrist along the ulna at the end of the extensor carpi ulnaris muscle.
ANATOMY: The branch of the medial antebrachial cutaneous nerve; more deeply, the posterior interosseous nerve.
METHOD: Strike or press this point against the ulnar bone. A strike will loosen the grip.

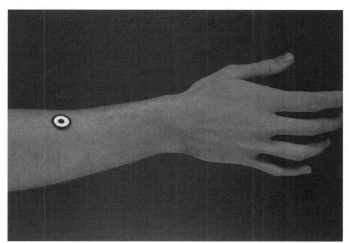

LARGE INTESTINE # 7: LI-7

LOCATION: About 5 AU up (proximal) from the wrist on the thumb side of the forearm.
ANATOMY: The posterior antebrachial cutaneous nerve and the deep ramus of the radial nerve.
METHOD: Strike this point against the bone, in the direction of the hand.
NOTE: LI-7 and L-6 (above) are in the same relative position on the forearm, on either side of the radius, and serve similar functions. Typically, yin points on the arm, such as L-6, are more sensitive than yang points. So, if an opponent grabs your lapel with one hand, strike L-6. However, when the opponent grabs with two hands, the arm yin points become less active, and the yang points become hyper-active. Under those circumstances strike LI-7.

LARGE INTESTINE # 10: LI-10

LOCATION: 2 AU distal from the outside end of the crease of the elbow (the lateral end of the transverse cubital crease), between the supinator longus muscle (also called the brachioradialus) and the extensor carpi radialis longus. It is approximately one AU down (distal) from the elbow joint on the outside of the forearm.

ANATOMY: The muscular branch of the musculo-spiral nerve, the antebrachial cutaneous nerve; a deep branch of the radial nerve.

METHOD: Striking this point will produce numbness in the arm, and cause an opponent's head to come forward, exposing head and neck points to follow-up attack. To practice, this point may be pressed with the thumb. [A]

NOTE: The numbness occurs because LI-10 is the motor-nerve point (the location where the nerve enters the muscle) of the extensor carpi radialis longus.

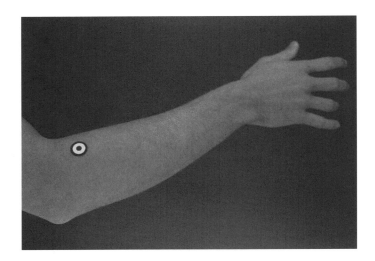

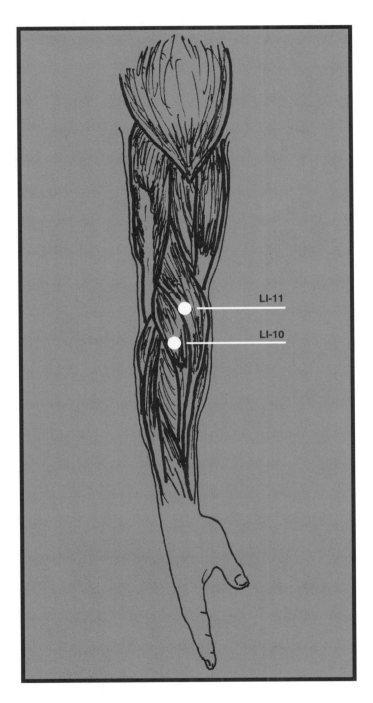

LI-11

LI-10

LARGE INTESTINE # 11: LI-11

LOCATION: On the radial aspect of the elbow, at the origin of the extensor carpi radialis muscle and the radial side of the brachioradialis muscle. This point can be found just to the outside of the crease of the elbow at the bulge of the muscle.

ANATOMY: The posterior cutaneous nerve and the radial nerve trunk.

METHOD: Strike this point back to front to produce numbness in the arm, and cause an opponent's head to come forward, exposing head and neck points to follow-up attack. This point may also be pressed with the thumb.

NOTE: The numbness occurs because LI-11 is the motor nerve point for the brachioradialis (supinator longus) muscle. Because of the close proximity and similar function of LI-10 and LI-11, these points are essentially interchangeable in kyusho-jitsu.

LUNG # 5: L-5

LOCATION: At the crease of the elbow, just outside (lateral) to the biceps tendon at the origin of the brachioradialis muscle.

ANATOMY: Branches of the radial recurrent artery and vein and the lateral cutaneous nerve of the forearm, directly above the main trunk of the radial nerve.

METHOD: Strike in a manner that cuts back towards the hand (think of a C-shaped movement), which will cause the knees to buckle, and the head to come forward. On some individuals, striking this target while pulling on the wrist points can send them to the ground, or even knock them unconscious [A-D]. This point may also be pressed with the tip of the thumb.

NOTE: There are actually three points in a row in this area, beginning with L-5 at the crease of the elbow, then moving down (distally) 2 AU to an "extraordinary" point labeled M-UE-31, then down one more AU to "extraordinary" point M-UE-32. These extraordinary points lie on branchings of the lateral cutaneous nerve of the forearm. References to L-5 should be understood as meaning any or all three of these points.

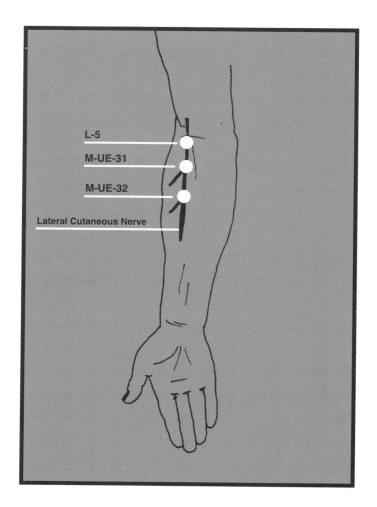

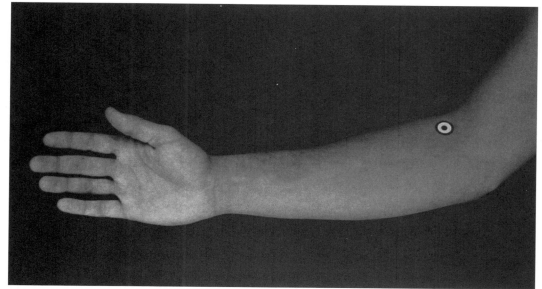

HEART # 3: H-3

LOCATION: In the pronator teres and the brachialis muscles, on the ulnar side of the elbow, just below (distal) the inner knob of the elbow (the medial condyle of the humerus).
ANATOMY: The medial cutaneous nerve of the forearm.
METHOD: Strike or press this point to bend the elbow and to numb the arm.

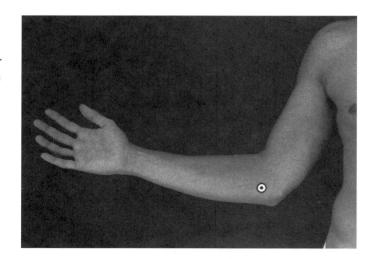

HEART # 2: H-2

LOCATION: Three AU above (proximal) the inside end of the crease of the elbow, in the space between the biceps and the triceps.
ANATOMY: The superior ulnar collateral artery, the medial antebrachial cutaneous nerve and the ulnar nerve.
METHOD: This point may be struck or grabbed causing the elbow to bend and pain to shoot down to the little finger (and sometimes up to the armpit). When grabbing this point, it is important to roll the thumb over the underlying nerves and tendons to cause greater pain.

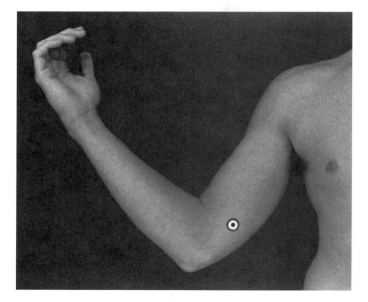

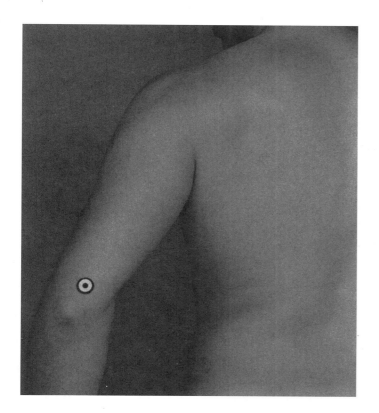

TRIPLE WARMER # 11: TW-11

LOCATION: Two AU above the tip of the elbow on the tendon of the triceps.

ANATOMY: The posterior brachial nerve, the muscular branch of the radial nerve, and the Body of Golgi's nerve receptor.

METHOD: Rub this point in and up and down motion to hyper-extend the elbow and lock the shoulder.

NOTE: This is a knead-point which lies over a tendon-nerve spindle called a Body of Golgi's. The function of the Body of Golgi's is to monitor the condition of the tendon. Rubbing this point tricks the mind into thinking that the tendon is tearing, which causes an immediate relaxation of the shoulder and the elbow.

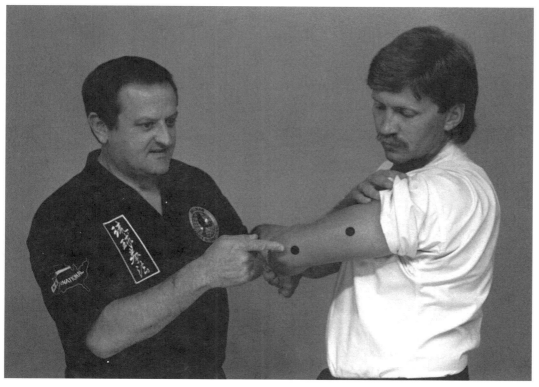

TRIPLE WARMER # 12: TW-12

LOCATION: In the middle of the triceps.

ANATOMY: The median collateral artery, the posterior brachial cutaneous nerve, and the muscular branch of the radial nerve. This point also lies over the fuciform fiber of the humerus bone.

METHOD: Strike this point against the bone to release the shoulder and lock the elbow.

NOTE: The fuciform fiber monitors the condition of the bone. A strike is interpreted as the humerus being in danger of breaking. As a result, the shoulder immediately releases, thereby enabling the elbow to be locked.

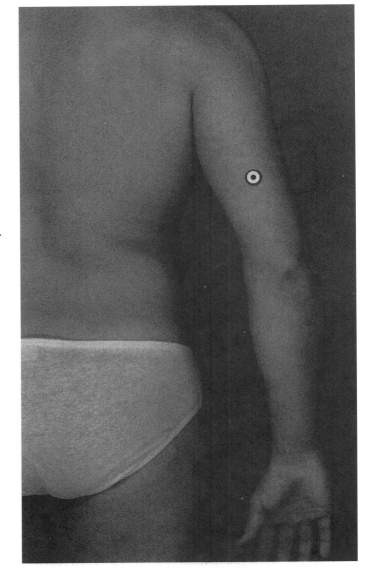

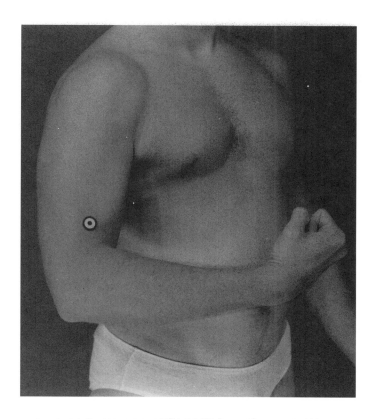

LARGE INTESTINE # 13: LI-13

LOCATION: In the hollow depression near the (distal) end of the biceps, about three AU above (proximal) the lateral epicondyle of the humerus (the outer knob of the elbow).

ANATOMY: The radial collateral artery, the posterior antebrachial cutaneous nerve and the radial nerve.

METHOD: Hit this point against the underlying bone (humerus) to bend the arm inward and cause numbing and pain down the arm to the end of the thumb. This point also responds to pressing.

PERICARDIUM # 2: P-2

LOCATION: Two AU below (distal) the level of the fold of the armpit (axillary crease) along the mid-line of the biceps.

ANATOMY: The muscular branches of the brachial artery, the medial brachial cutaneous nerve and the musculocutaneous nerve.

METHOD: This point can be struck straight-on to numb the biceps.

NOTE: In application against an opponent with long arms, it is possible to substitute "extraordinary" point N-UE-9, which is 2.5 AU below P-2, directly in the center of the biceps. [A]

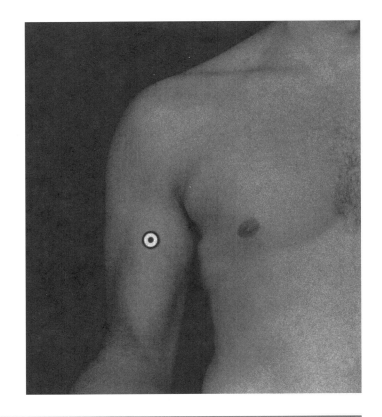

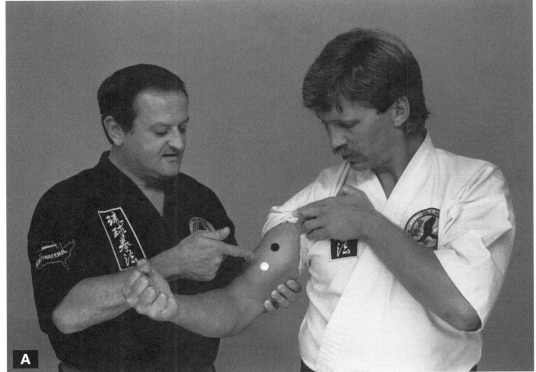

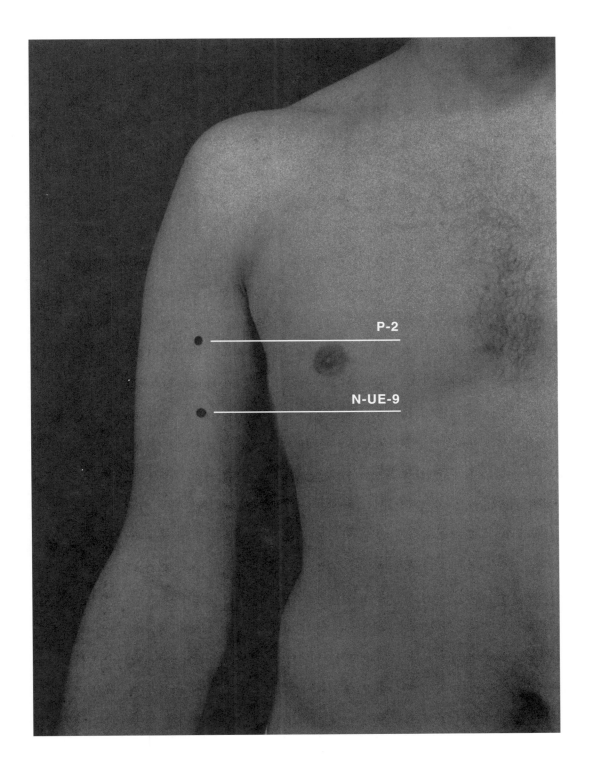

P-2

N-UE-9

Points of the head & neck

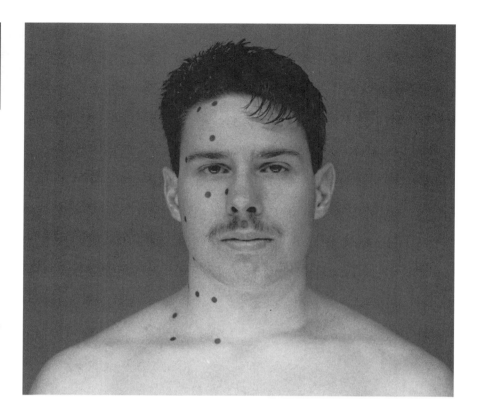

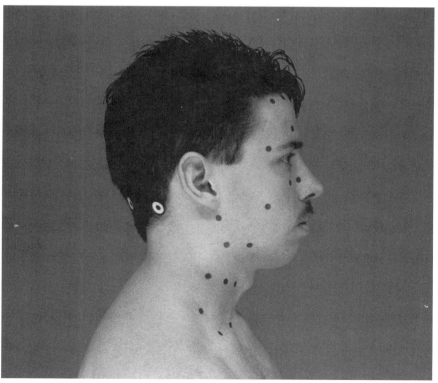

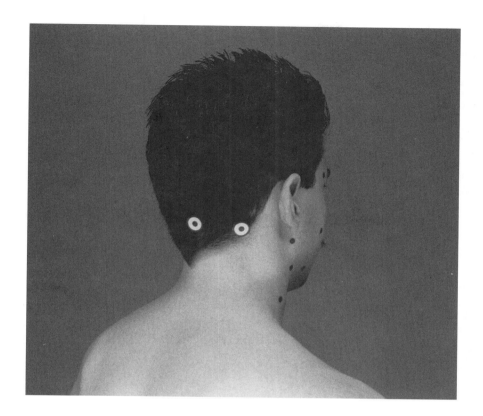

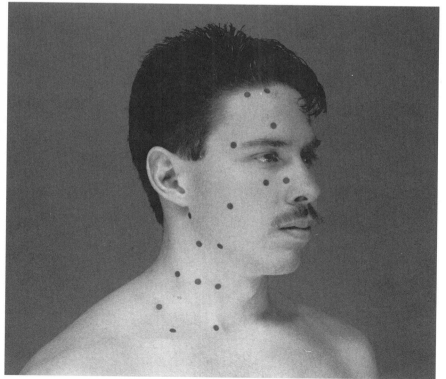

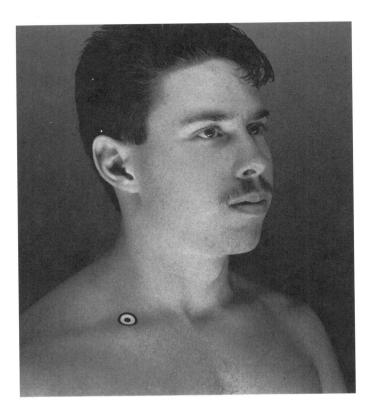

STOMACH # 12: S-12

LOCATION: In the depression at the middle of the superior border of the clavicle, 4 AU from the median line, at the clavicular head of the sternocleidomastoid muscle. This point lies just behind the collar-bone directly above the nipple.

ANATOMY: The transverse cervical artery, the intermediate, supraclavicular nerve, and the supraclavicular portion of the brachial plexus.

METHOD: Press downward behind the collar bone with the fingertips to drive the opponent to the ground. [A-E]

NOTE: According to the most ancient acupuncture texts, this point is the intersection point of the three arm yang meridians: small intestine, triple warmer, large intestine. This means that S-12 can be treated as another point on those meridians.

A

STOMACH # 11: S-11

LOCATION: At the medial superior border of the clavicle, at the depression just lateral to the sternal head of the sternocleidomastoid muscle. It is in the hollow just behind the collar-bone, next to the sternal notch.
ANATOMY: The anterior jugular vein, the common carotid artery, the medial supraclavicular nerve and the muscular branch of the ansa hypoglossi.
METHOD: Press with a fingertip in and down to drop an opponent.

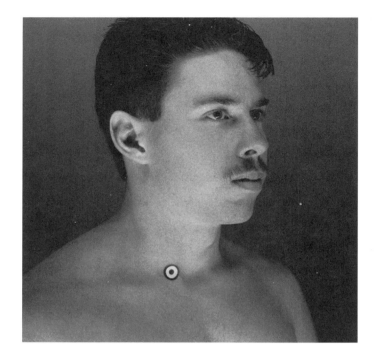

LARGE INTESTINE # 17: LI-17

LOCATION: On the lateral aspect of the neck, 2 AU above S-12, between the posterior border of the sternocleidomastoid and the anterior border of the trapezius. It is in the hollow triangle between the two muscles on the side of the neck, where the neck rises from the body.
ANATOMY: The external jugular vein, the cutaneous cervical nerve, and the phrenic nerve.
METHOD: Strike this point at a downward diagonal angle to disrupt the lungs. Even a light blow can cause an episode of uncontrollable coughing.

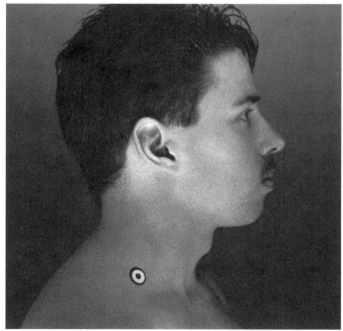

Jack Hogan of Jacksonville, Florida, (far left) knocks out Jason Moore with a knuckle tap to stomach point 9 from kata Nai Hanchi.

STOMACH # 9: S-9

LOCATION: At the meeting of the anterior border of the sternocleidomastoid and the thyroid cartilage, level with the laryngeal prominence. It is level with the Adam's apple, at the crease of the neck muscle.
ANATOMY: The bifurcation of the carotid arteries, the cutaneous colli nerve, a cervical branch of the facial (seventh cranial) nerve, and the vagus nerve.
METHOD: Strike with a penetrating blow on a 45 degree angle into the neck to produce unconsciousness. [A-D]

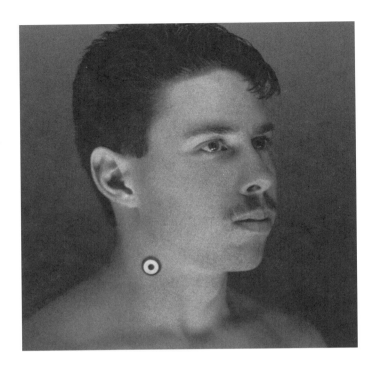

LARGE INTESTINE # 18: LI-18

LOCATION: 3 AU lateral to the laryngeal prominence, in the posterior margin of the sternocleidomastoid.
It can be found on the side of the neck, level with the Adam's apple and directly below the ear.
ANATOMY: The ascending cervical artery, the great auricular nerve, the cutaneous colli nerve, the lesser occipital nerve and the accessory nerve.
METHOD: Touch LI-18 on one side of the neck while striking LI-18 on the opposite side. The direction of force is on a line connecting LI-18 on both sides of the neck. [A-D]

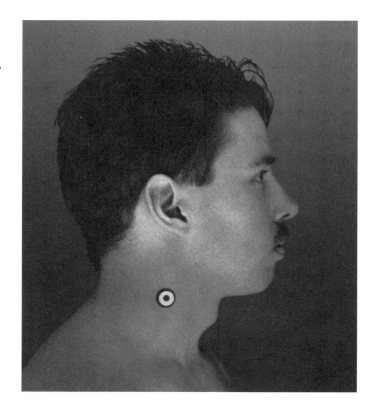

SMALL INTESTINE # 16: SI-16

LOCATION: On the posterior border of the sternoclei-domastoid, 1 AU posterior to LI-18. This point lies on the side of the neck, level with the Adam's apple, and just behind the muscle.

ANATOMY: The ascending cervical artery, the cutaneous cervical nerve, and the emerging portion of the great auricular nerve.

METHOD: With the opponent's head turned slightly, strike this point at about a 30 degree angle from back to front. [A-C]

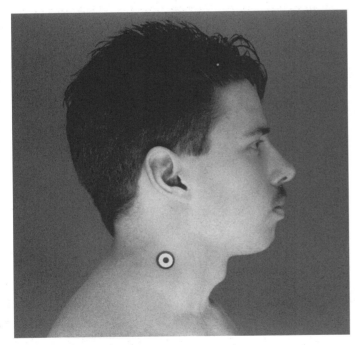

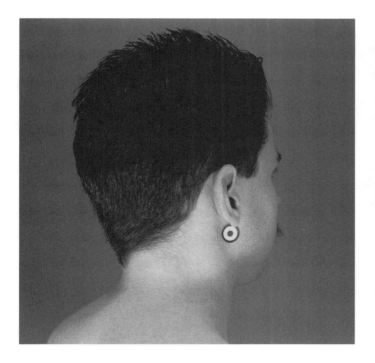

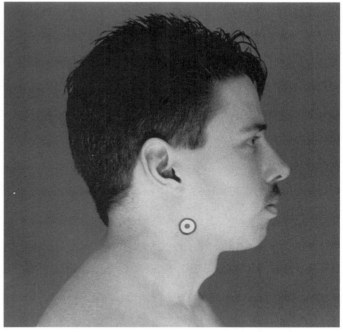

TRIPLE WARMER # 17: TW-17

LOCATION: Behind the jaw, in the depression under the ear.

ANATOMY: The posterior auricular artery, the superficial jugular vein, the great auricular nerve and the facial (seventh cranial) nerve at its point of emergence from the stylomastoid foramen.

METHOD: Strike diagonally back to front, hitting the point against the back of the jaw-bone, resulting in unconsciousness.

WARNING: A blow at this point can dislocate the jaw.

SMALL INTESTINE # 17: SI-17

LOCATION: Posterior to the angle of the mandible in the anterior margin at the insertion of the sternocleidomastoid muscle. It is located in the depression behind the corner of the jaw.

ANATOMY: The internal carotid artery, a branch of the great auricular nerve, a cervical branch of the facial (seventh cranial) nerve, and a superior cervical ganglion of the sympathetic trunk.

METHOD: This point is poked or pressed on an upward 45 degree angle toward the center of the head. [A]

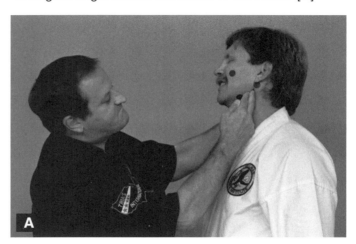

STOMACH # 5: S-5

LOCATION: Anterior to the angle of the mandible, on the anterior border of the masseter muscle, at the groove of the jaw. It is found at the notch along the bottom of the jaw.

ANATOMY: The facial artery and the buccal nerve.

METHOD: Hit this point on a line 45 degrees towards the center of the head. Single knuckle or finger-tip strikes should roll into the inside of the bone. Palm strikes hit on the groove of the jaw with a slight twisting motion.

NOTE: In self-defense, students are commonly taught to execute a palm strike against the point of the jaw. But, that is an ineffective technique. [A] However, by striking S-5 with the proper angle and direction, an opponent can be easily knocked out. [B, C]

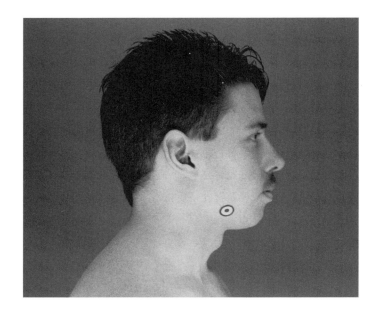

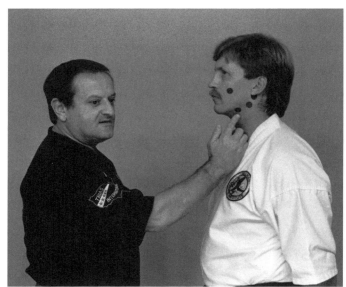

A. Ineffective technique.

B &C. Proper technique.

Note: Use the left hand on your opponent's right (jaw) side and your right hand on his left (jaw) side.

SMALL INTESTINE # 18: SI-18

LOCATION: At the mid-point of the inferior margin of the zygomatic bone, directly below the outer canthus of the eye. It lies in the depression below the prominence of the cheekbone, in front of the masseter (the muscle which bulges when clenching the jaw).

ANATOMY: The transverse facial artery, the facial (seventh cranial) nerve and the infraorbital nerve.

METHOD: This point is struck or pressed on an upward diagonal line towards the center of the head causing the neck to release. [A]

NOTE: A preferred method of attacking this point is with middle knuckle fist (nakadaka ken), which is formed by allowing the second joint of the middle finger to protrude like a spear-head. This particular fist is suited for delivering upward energy. [B-D]

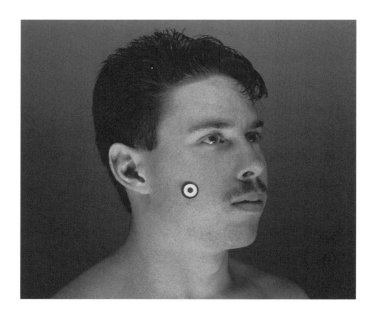

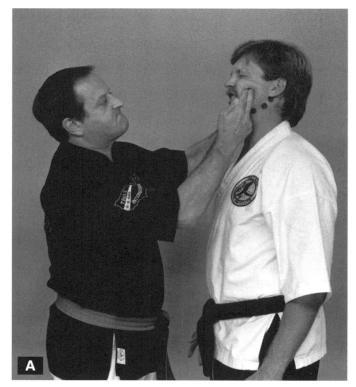

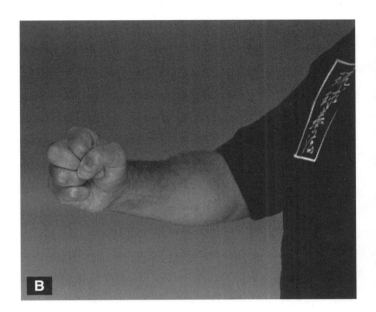

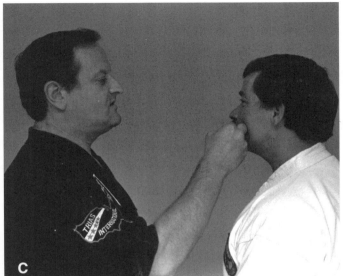

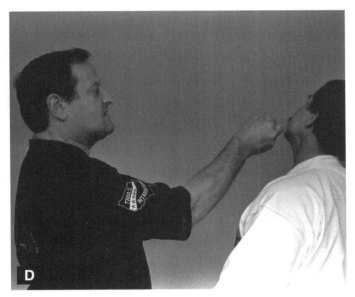

GALL BLADDER FRONTAL CLUSTER

On the forehead above the eye are three points which can be reached with one hand. This cluster is the preferred target for the top hand in morote-waza (two-handed techniques) such as the double palm heel smash.

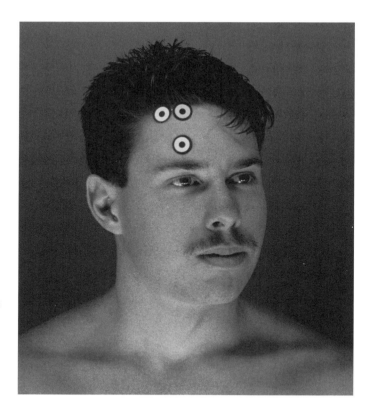

GALL BLADDER # 14: GB-14

LOCATION: In the frontalis muscle, 1 AU above the mid-point of the eyebrow, in the depression of the superciliary arch. It is directly above the pupil of the eye (eyes looking straight ahead) about one third of the distance from the eyebrow to the top of the forehead.
ANATOMY: Situated directly on a lateral branch of the frontal nerve.

GALL BLADDER # 15: GB-15

LOCATION: Above GB-14, just in the hairline.
ANATOMY: Anastomotic branch of the medial and lateral branches of the frontal nerve.

GALL BLADDER # 13: GB-13

LOCATION: In the hairline, 1 AU to the side of GB-14, in the lateral aspect of the forehead.
ANATOMY: The lateral branch of the frontal nerve.
METHOD: Strike these points with a palm technique to cause motor impairment and disorientation leading to unconsciousness.

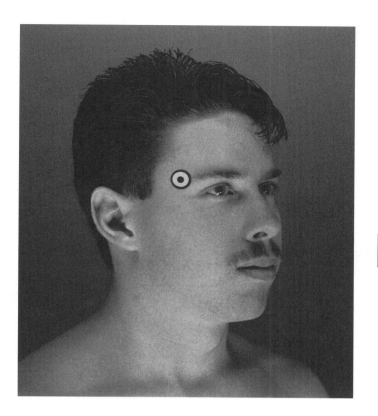

TRIPLE WARMER # 23: TW-23

LOCATION: In the oricularis oculi muscle, on the lateral border of the zygomatic process of the frontal bone. It is at the end of the eyebrow in the depression of the temple.

ANATOMY: The zygomaticotemporalis nerve.

METHOD: Strike with a small surface, such as a middle- knuckle fist, from the side, and slightly forward.

NOTE: TW-23 is the terminus point of the triple warmer meridian.

WARNING: Never actually strike this point in practice.

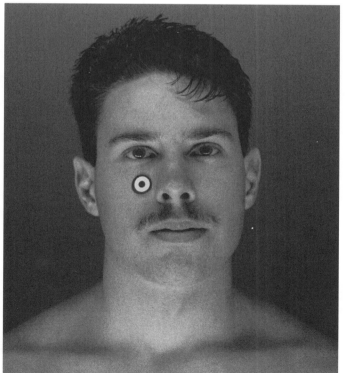

STOMACH # 2: S-2

LOCATION: 1 AU directly below the pupil at the crest of the cheekbone.

ANATOMY: This point is situated directly on the infraorbital foramen.

METHOD: Strike with a slightly downward motion.

GOVERNOR # 26: GV-26

LOCATION: The philtrum, in the orbicularis oris muscle. It is located in the depression between the nose and the upper lip.

ANATOMY: A buccal branch of the facial (seventh cranial) nerve and a branch of the infraorbital nerve.

METHOD: Contrary to popular teaching, this is not a hit-point. Rather it is a rub-point. Rub with a lateral motion using the foreknuckles of the fist to control the opponent's head. It can be used to drive away an attacker, [A, B] or, with one hand grasping the hair, and the other rubbing Gv-26, to apply a neck wrenching technique.

NOTE: The large intestine meridian is unique among all meridians in that it crosses the centerline of the body. The terminus point, LI-20, of the right side large intestine meridian is located at the left edge of the nose, and similarly the left LI meridian ends on the right side of the nose. The point at which the right and left meridians cross the centerline is Gv-26.

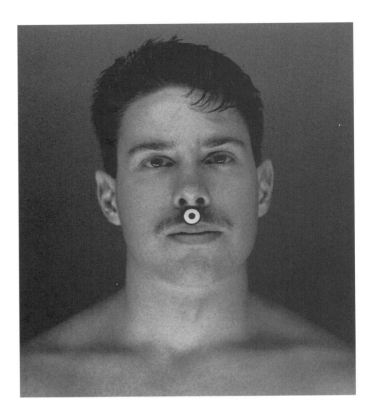

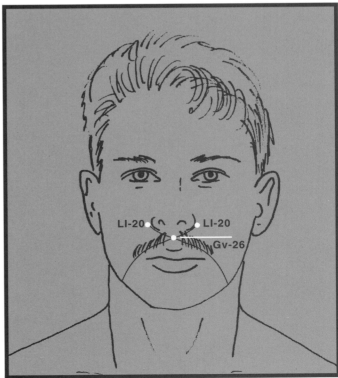

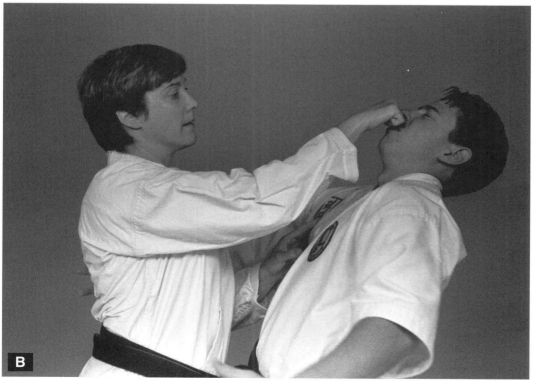

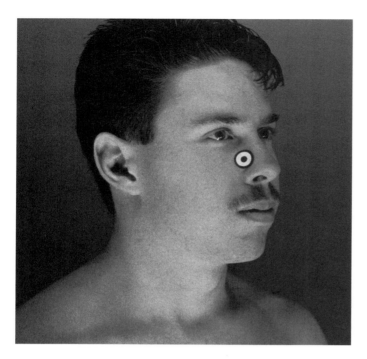

M-HN-14:

LOCATION: At the lateral, inferior side of the nasal bone, at the superior end of the nasolabial sulcus. It is on the side of the nose, just at the juncture of the nose and the cheek.

ANATOMY: The anterior ethmoidal nerve, the infratrochlearis nerve, and a branch of the infraorbital nerve.

METHOD: Strike this point from the side to cause the eyes to close tightly and immediately tear up. A substantial blow will break the nose.

NOTE: Commonly, students are taught to strike directly against the bridge of the nose. [A, B] While undoubtedly painful, the nose is structurally strongest straight on. Only a blow from the side against this pressure point can cause damage with minimal effort. [C-F]

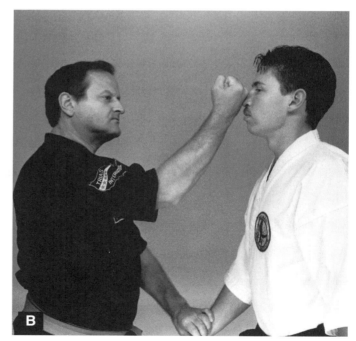

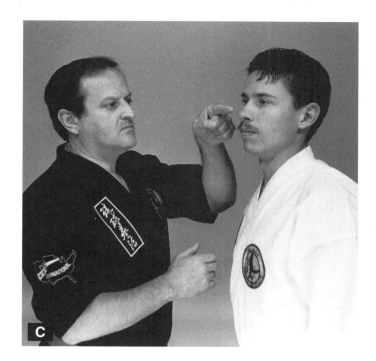

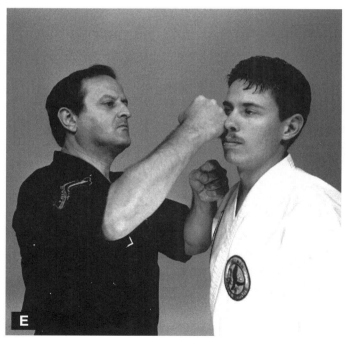

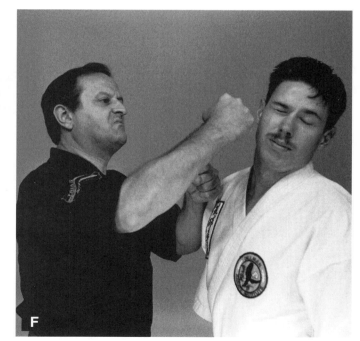

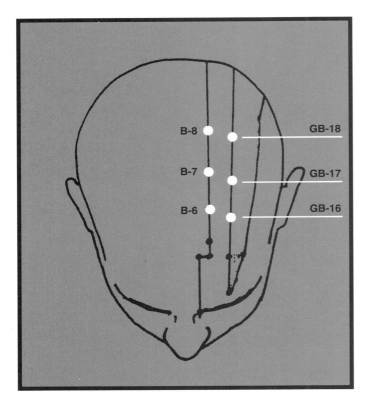

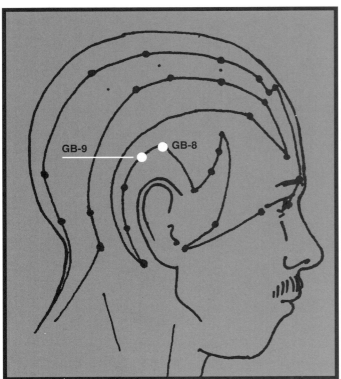

SCALP POINT CLUSTER

GALL BLADDER # 16, 17, 18:

LOCATION: In the scalp, along the curve of the skull, 2 AU either side of the centerline.
ANATOMY: Branches of the frontal and great occipital nerves.

BLADDER # 6, 7, 8:

LOCATION: In the scalp, along the curve of the skull, 1 AU either side of the centerline. [A] p. 111
ANATOMY: Branches of the frontal and the great occipital nerves.

GALL BLADDER # 8, 9:

LOCATION: In the scalp, along a curved line 1.5 AU supraposterior to the ear. These points are located above and behind the ear on the back quarter of the skull.
ANATOMY: Branches of the great occipital nerve.
NOTE: These are substitute points for the bladder and gall bladder points mentioned above, and should be used on individuals with baldness or thinning hair on the top of the head.

METHOD: Rub these points (children have long known these points as the place for giving "nuggies"), or grab the hair, digging the knuckles into the scalp. [B] p.111.
NOTE: When using any of the above scalp points, it is necessary to rub or dig with the knuckles. [A-C] p.112. When grabbing pull the hair taut and dig into the pressure points with the foreknuckles of the fist. [A-D] p.113.

GRABBING AT GB-16 & B-6

GRABBING AT GB-8 & GB-9

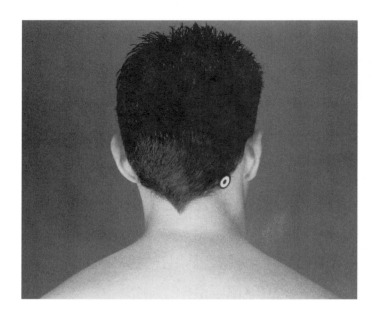

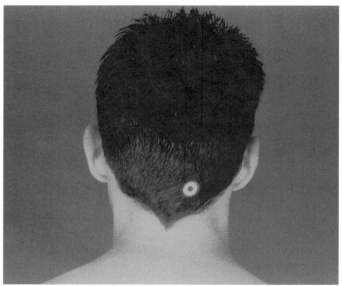

GALL BLADDER # 20: GB-20

LOCATION: In the hollow at the back of neck (between the trapezius and sternocleidomastoid muscles), just below the occipital bone.
ANATOMY: A branch of the lesser occipital nerve.
METHOD: Strike this point from back to front to produce unconsciousness. A light blow will cause a tingling sensation down the back of the body to the feet, typically causing the heels to pull off the ground.

BLADDER # 10: B-10

LOCATION: At the base of the skull, 1 AU lateral to the first cervical vertebrae, at the origin of the trapezius muscle.
ANATOMY: The trunk of the great occipital nerve.
METHOD: Strike this point from back to front with a slightly rising motion to knock an opponent to the ground.

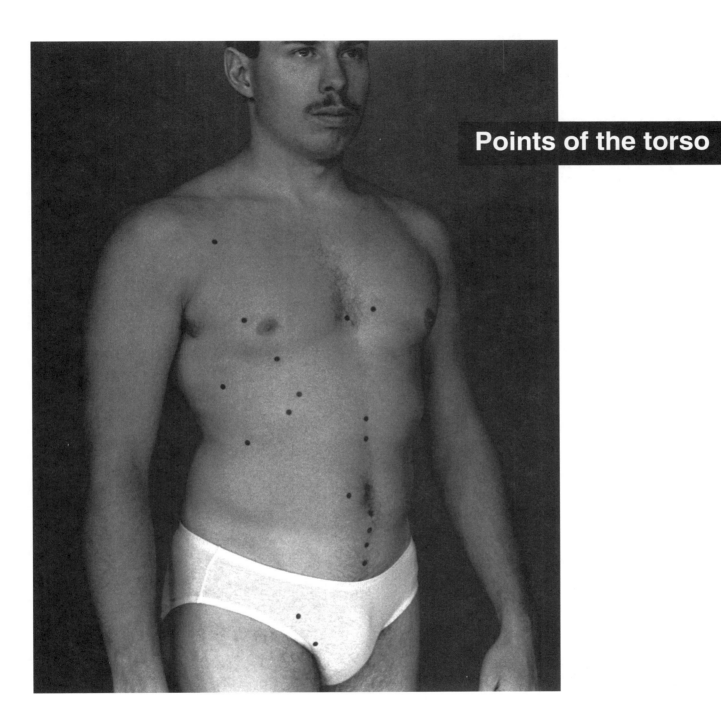

Points of the torso

LUNG # 1: L-1

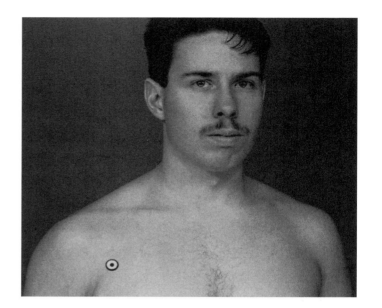

LOCATION: In the upper portion of the pectoralis muscle, about 1 AU below the lateral end of the clavicle in the first intercostal space. It is on a line about halfway between the axillary (armpit) and the top of the shoulder, on the curve of the upper chest near the meeting of the chest and shoulder.

ANATOMY: An intermediate branch of the supraclavicular nerve, a branch of the anterior thoracic nerve and the first intercostal nerve.

METHOD: Strike this point in a downward and inward direction to disrupt the respiratory system.

NOTE: L-1 is the alarm point for the lung meridian, which (from the point of view of kyusho-jitsu) makes it a particularly vulnerable point.

PERICARDIUM # 1: P-1

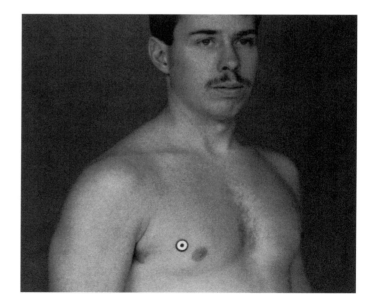

LOCATION: In the fourth intercostal space, 1 AU supralateral to the nipple. It is just to the outside and above the nipple in the space between the 4th and 5th ribs.

ANATOMY: The muscular branch of the anterior thoracic nerve and the 4th intercostal nerve.

METHOD: Strike this point on a line towards the center of the back.

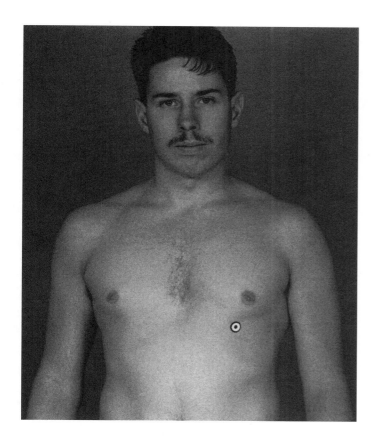

STOMACH # 18: S-18

LOCATION: Below the nipple in the fifth intercostal space, at the lower margin of the pectoralis muscle.
ANATOMY: The branch fifth intercostal nerve.
METHOD: Punch this point directly.
NOTE: The pectoralis muscle is a poor target because of its mass, particularly on body-builders. However, just below the muscle, at S-18, the body is vulnerable, especially on those who have stretched and lifted the nerves by over-developing the muscle. Further, S-18 is a point where an electrode is attached during a twelve-lead EKG.

RIB CAGE BORDER CLUSTER

At the border of the rib cage and abdomen are two points, Li-14 and GB-24, which work together very effectively. These two points are a common target for the lower hand in two-handed techniques.

LIVER # 14: Li-14

LOCATION: At the medial margin of the rib cage at the merging of the sixth and seventh costal cartilage.
ANATOMY: The sixth intercostal nerve.
NOTE: Li-14 is the alarm point for the liver meridian as well as a linking point between the liver and spleen meridians.

GALL BLADDER # 24: GB-24

LOCATION: At the medial margin of the rib cage at the merging of the seventh and eighth costal cartilage.
ANATOMY: The seventh intercostal nerve.
NOTE: This is the alarm point for the gallbladder meridian, as well as a linking point between the gallbladder and bladder meridians.

METHOD: Strike these points diagonally up and in.
NOTE: These points are particularly potent because a strike here affects both yin (liver and spleen) and yang (gallbladder and bladder) simultaneously.

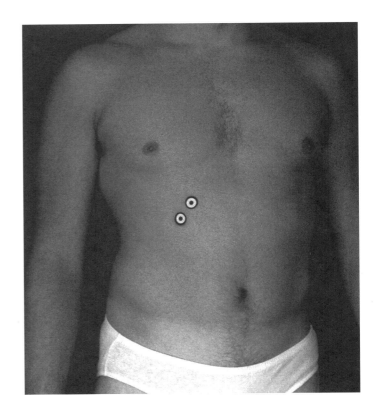

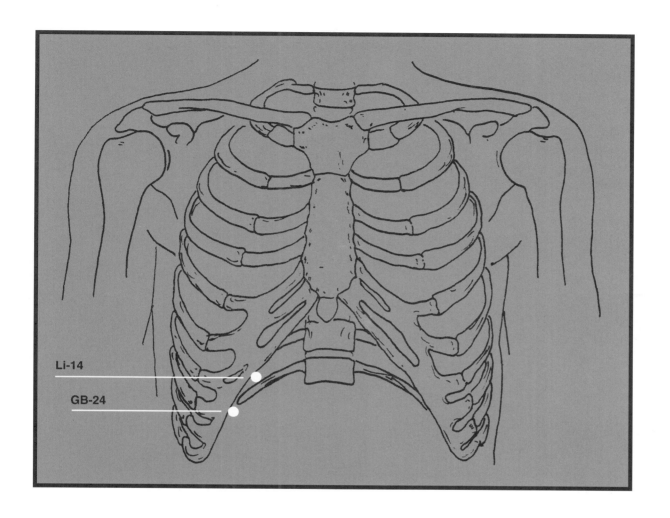

Li-14

GB-24

CONCEPTION # 17: CO-17

LOCATION: On the sternum, level with the nipples, and just above the articulations of the right and left fifth rib and the sternum.
ANATOMY: A medial anterior cutaneous branch of the fourth intercostal nerve.
METHOD: Punch this point directly.
NOTE: This is the alarm point of the pericardium meridian, and the intersection point of the spleen, kidney, small intestine and triple warmer meridians on the conception channel. It is considered one of eight influential points dominating ki. It also lies directly over the heart.

WARNING: A blow to the sternum at this point can damage the heart.

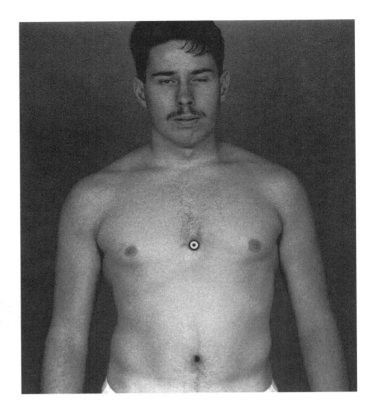

KIDNEY # 23: K-23

LOCATION: In the fourth intercostal space, 2 AU lateral to the mid-line. This point is level with the nipples and Co-17, just to either side of the sternum.
ANATOMY: Fourth intercostal nerve, as well as an anterior cutaneous branch of the same.
METHOD: Strike this point directly, typically with a single-knuckle fist (ippon-ken). [A]
NOTE: On the left side this point lies directly over the heart.

WARNING: Do not strike this point in practice.

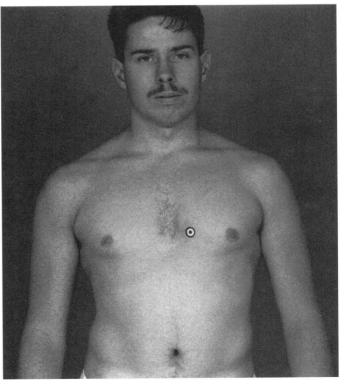

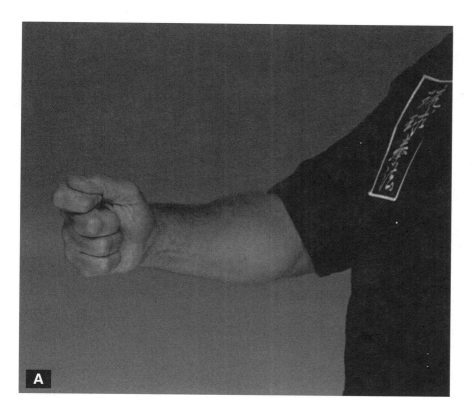

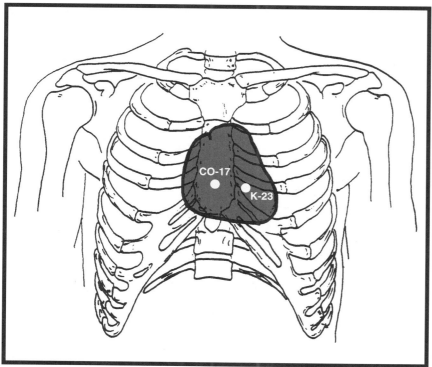

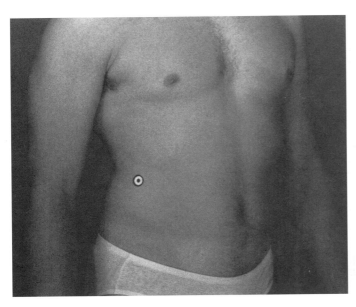

LIVER # 13: Li-13

LOCATION: In the internal and external oblique muscles at the anterior end of the eleventh rib. This point can be located at the free end of the longer of the two floating ribs, at about the place the elbow touches the side of the body.
ANATOMY: The tenth intercostal nerve.
METHOD: Strike this point diagonally upward.
NOTE: Li-13 is the alarm point of the spleen meridian. This point contains an internal cycle of destruction as it relates to both the liver (wood) and spleen (earth) meridians.

WARNING: Do not strike this point in practice.

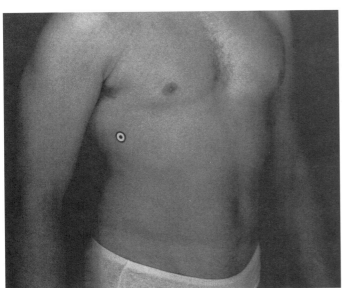

SPLEEN # 21: SP-21

LOCATION: On the mid-axillary line, in the seventh intercostal space. This point can be found on the side of the body, midway between the center of the armpit and the free end of the eleventh (floating) rib.
ANATOMY: The seventh intercostal nerve and the terminal branch of the long thoracic nerve.
METHOD: Strike this point from the side towards the body-center.

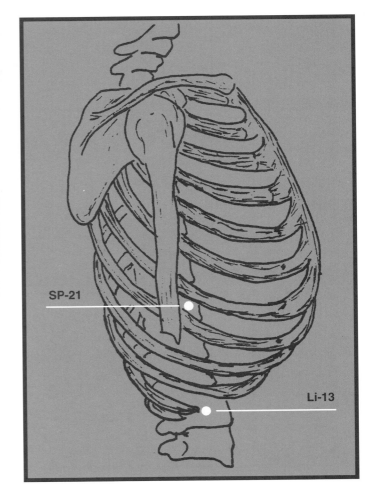

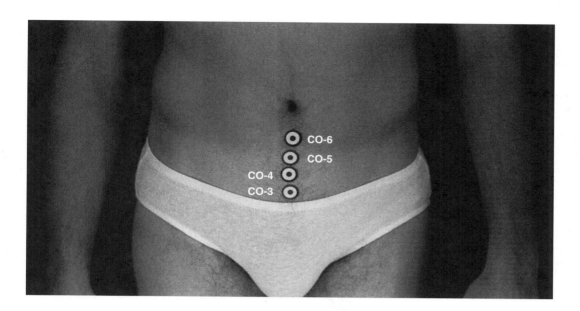

TANDEN CLUSTER

The tanden, or "ki-center" is the source of intrinsic energy for the body. Along the centerline, over the tanden are four important points. These points include the main tanden point (Co-6) as well as three "alarm" points.

CONCEPTION # 6: CO-6

LOCATION: 1.5 AU directly below the navel on the median line of the body.
ANATOMY: A medial anterior branch of the eleventh intercostal nerve.
NOTE: The oriental name for Co-6 is kikai, "Sea of Ki" This point is the ki center (tanden) of the body.

CONCEPTION # 5: CO-5

LOCATION: 2 AU directly below the navel.
ANATOMY: A medial anterior cutaneous branch of the intercostal nerve.
NOTE: Co-5 is the alarm point for the triple warmer meridian.

CONCEPTION # 4: CO-4

LOCATION: 3 AU directly below the navel.
ANATOMY: A medial anterior cutaneous branch of the intercostal nerve.
NOTE: Co-4 is the alarm point of the small intestine meridian.

CONCEPTION # 3: CO-3

LOCATION: 4 AU directly below the navel on the median line of the body.
ANATOMY: A branch of the iliohypogastric nerve.
NOTE: Co-3 is the alarm point of the bladder meridian. It is also the point at which the three leg yin meridians (kidney, spleen and liver) intersect on the conception meridian.
METHOD: Strike these points either diagonally downward or diagonally upward to incapacitate an opponent.
CAUTION: Three classics of Chinese acupuncture — "The Great Compendium", "Bronze Statue" and "The Glorious Anthology of Acupuncture" — state the Co-5 should not be needled on women or they will be "rendered incapable of bearing children for life" (*Fundamentals of Chinese Acupuncture*). For this reason, we advise that techniques directed against the tanden collection of points only be indicated in practice with women.

Points of the lower extremities

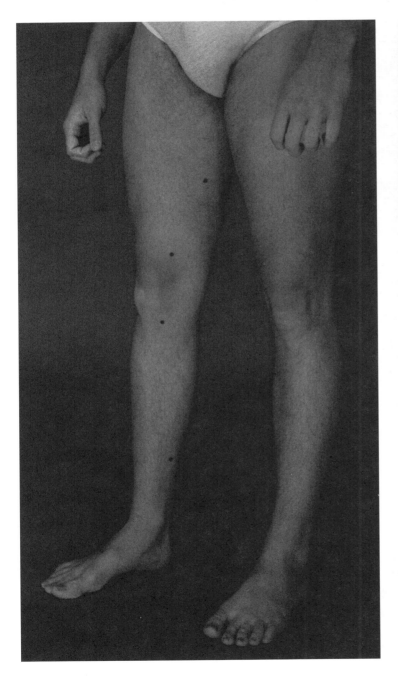
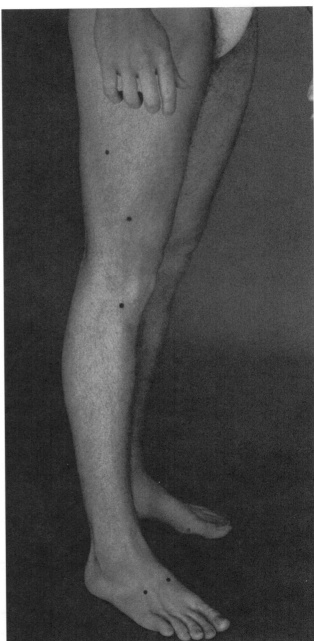

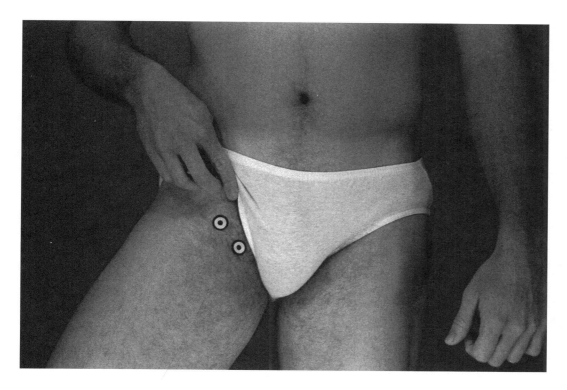

INGUINAL CREASE CLUSTER

In the inguinal crease, the border between the thigh and the hip, just lateral to the crotch, lie the points Li-12 and Sp-12. Liver is a wood meridian and spleen is an earth meridian. Since wood "penetrates" earth, these points work together according to the law of destruction.

LIVER # 12: Li-12

LOCATION: Level with the pubic symphysis, 2.5 AU either side of the centerline, in the inguinal groove. It is located in the crease found at the border of the upper thigh and the hips.

ANATOMY: The ilioinguinal nerve, and the anterior branch of the obturator nerve.

SPLEEN #12: SP-12

LOCATION: Level with the upper border of the pubic symphysis, 3.5 AU lateral to the centerline, in the crease of the leg. It is lccated just at the outside edge of the femoral artery.

ANATOMY: The point at which the femoral nerve traverses.

METHOD: Strike these points diagonally downward, on a path that moves slightly outward. Attacks to this area will cause an opponent to bend over, and expose points on the back of the head to attack (see pages 57-58).

SPLEEN # 11: SP-11

LOCATION: Posterior to the sartorius muscle, on the medial aspect of the thigh, about midway between the knee-joint and the groin. This point is located in the middle of the inner thigh.

ANATOMY: The anterior femoral cutaneous nerve and the saphenous nerve.

METHOD: Strike this point to buckle the leg and knock an opponent to the ground. [A-C]

NOTE: Typically, this point is struck with a toe-tip kick (tsumasaki-geri). [D] A story told about karate master Arakaki Ankichi illustrates the use of this technique. Apparently Arakaki's brother once bet him that he could take one of the master's kicks. Arakakai, using his toe-tip, kicked his brother in the thigh. The brother became sick with a fever and a few days later required surgery on his thigh. Though the story does not indicate which vital point Arakaki attacked, Sp-11 is likely the one. In similar fashion, some hours after the photograph detailing this kick was taken, the "victim" became ill, requiring the application of energy restoration techniques by George Dillman. Readers are urged to refrain from kicking this point.

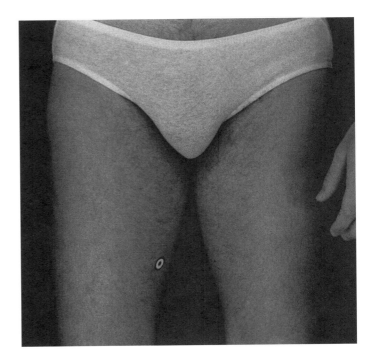

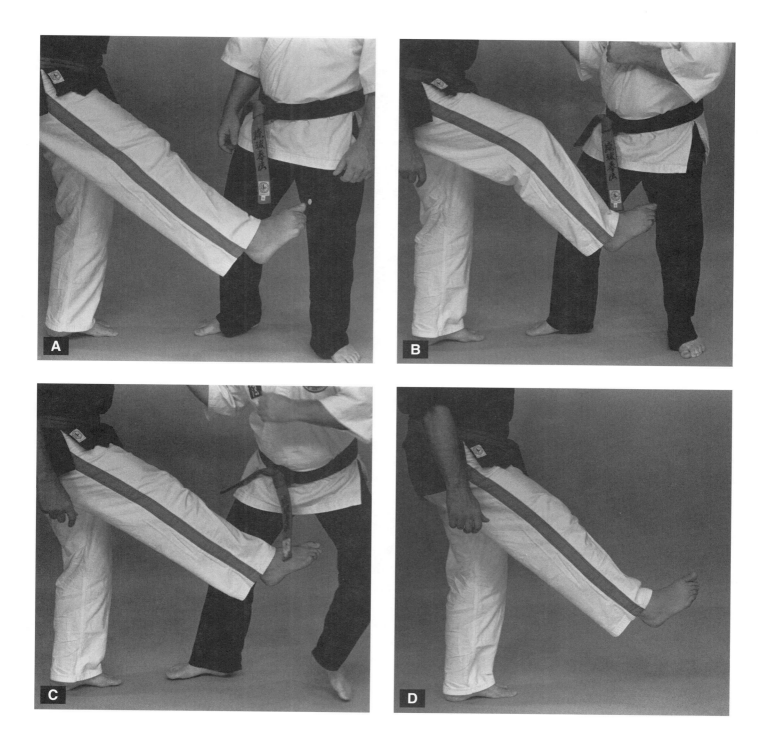

GALL BLADDER # 31: GB-31

LOCATION: Beneath the tensor fasciae latae, in the vastus lateralis muscle, at the median line of the lateral aspect of the thigh, 7 AU above the knee. This can be found by standing upright with the arm extended along the side of the leg. GB-31 will be just at the tip of the middle finger. [DIAGRAM]
ANATOMY: The lateral cutaneous nerve of the thigh, and a muscular branch of the femoral nerve.
METHOD: Strike this point from the side.
NOTE: This is a motor-nerve point, and the favorite target of the Muay Thai shin kick. Children often knee this point on each other while calling out, "Charlie horse."

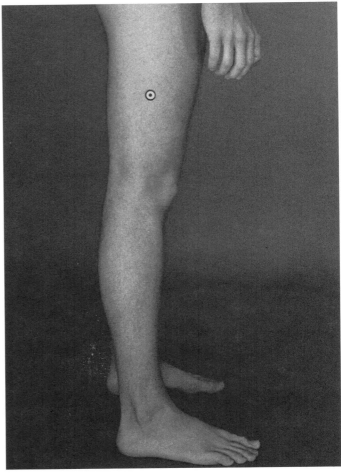

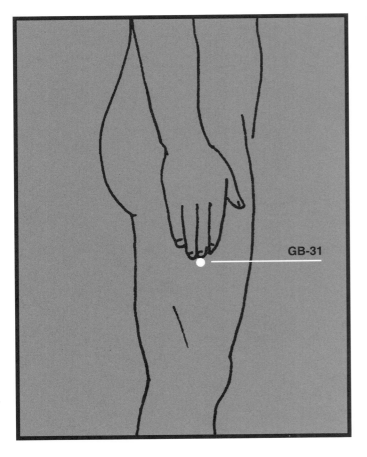

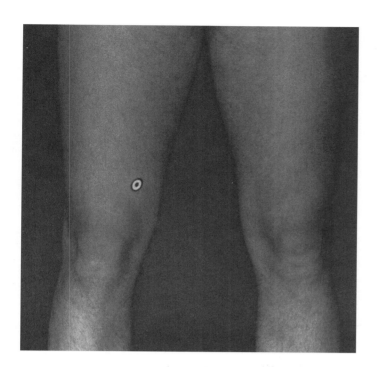

SPLEEN # 10: SP-10

LOCATION: At the superior margin of the medial condyle of the femur, in the medial margin of the vastus medialis muscle. This point is on the inner aspect of the leg, about 3 AU above the level of the knee-cap.
ANATOMY: The anterior femoral cutaneous nerve, and a muscular branch of the femoral nerve.
METHOD: Strike diagonally downward following an imaginary line through the center of the knee to dislocate the joint and/or knock the opponent to the ground.

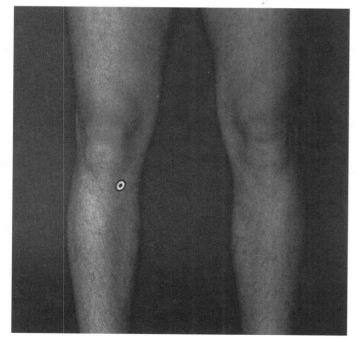

SPLEEN # 9: SP-9

LOCATION: In the depression between the posterior margin of the tibia and the gastrocnemius muscle, at the origin of the soleus. This point is on the inner aspect of the knee about 2 AU below the knee-cap.
ANATOMY: A cutaneous branch of the saphenous nerve, and the tibial nerve.
METHOD: Strike diagonally upward on a line through the center of the knee to dislocate the joint and/or knock the opponent to the ground.

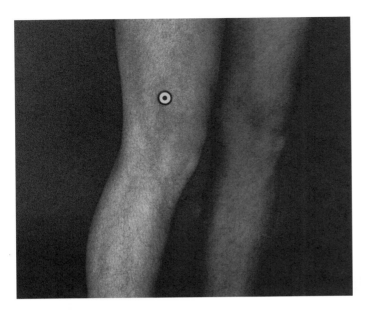

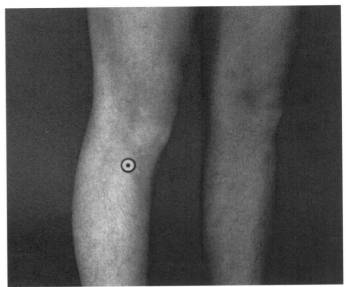

STOMACH # 34: S-34

LOCATION: On the lateral aspect of the thigh in the vastus lateralis muscle, at the border of the vastus medialis muscle. This point is about 3 AU above the knee-cap on the outside of the thigh.
ANATOMY: This point is situated directly on the lateral femoral cutaneous nerve.
METHOD: Strike diagonally downward on a line through the center of the knee to dislocate the joint and/or knock the opponent to the ground.

N-LE-7

LOCATION: About 3 AU below the knee lateral to the tibia in the tibialis anterior muscle.
ANATOMY: The lateral cutaneous nerve of the calf, a cutaneous branch of the saphenous nerve and the deep peroneal nerve.
METHOD: Strike this point diagonally upward through the center of the knee to dislocate the joint and/or knock the opponent to the ground.

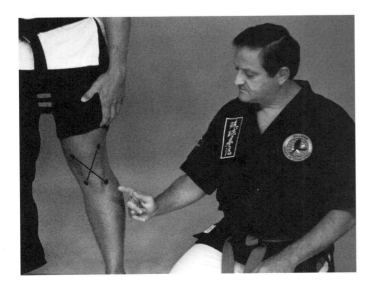

NOTE ON FOUR KNEE POINTS: When striking with a very small surface (such as a knuckle) accurate placement is essential in order to effortlessly use these points to knock an opponent down. [A, B] However, when kicking, a shorthand method can be used for locating them: Simply envision an "X" drawn across the knee, and attack the ends of the "X" on an imaginary line which passes through the center of the joint.

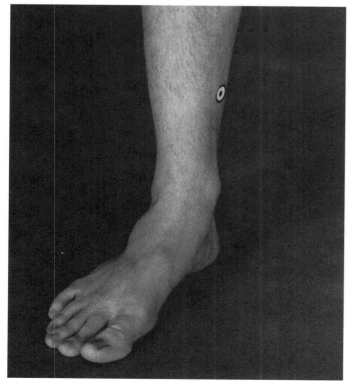

SPLEEN # 6: SP-6

LOCATION: Between the posterior margin of the tibia and the soleus muscle, 3 AU above the medial malleolus of the ankle. It is on the inside of the leg, just along the rear edge of the bone (tibia) about midway between the prominence of the ankle and the lower edge of the calf muscle.

ANATOMY: A cutaneous branch of the saphenous nerve, and the tibial nerve.

METHOD: Kick this point from the inside with a rising motion to rob the leg of energy.

NOTE: Sp-6 is named Sanyinjiao, "the meeting of the three yins." At this point, the kidney and liver meridians cross the spleen meridian, forming an intersection of the three leg yin meridians. Sp-6 can function as a part of all three meridians; so it is commonly used to set-up other points.

GALL BLADDER # 41: GB-41

LOCATION: In the depression just in front of the merging of the fourth and fifth metatarsal bones. It is located just in front of the bulge on the top of the foot where the bones of the fourth and fifth toes connect.
ANATOMY: The dorsal digital nerve of the fourth metatarsus.
METHOD: Stomp this point. If an opponent is shoeless and kicking, GB-41 may also be struck with a single knuckle.

LIVER # 3: Li-3

LOCATION: In the depression between the first and second metatarsals. This point can be found on the top of the foot, between the two bones leading to the first (big) and second toes.
ANATOMY: The peroneal nerve.
METHOD: Press or strike this point diagonally downward.
NOTE: Li-3 is best used when the opponent's feet are unshod, or in lightweight shoes.

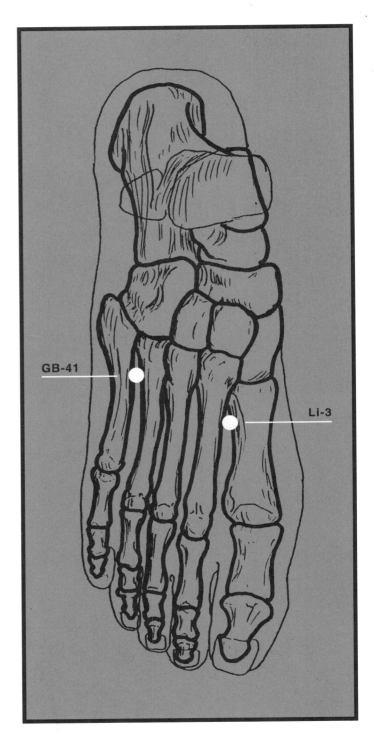

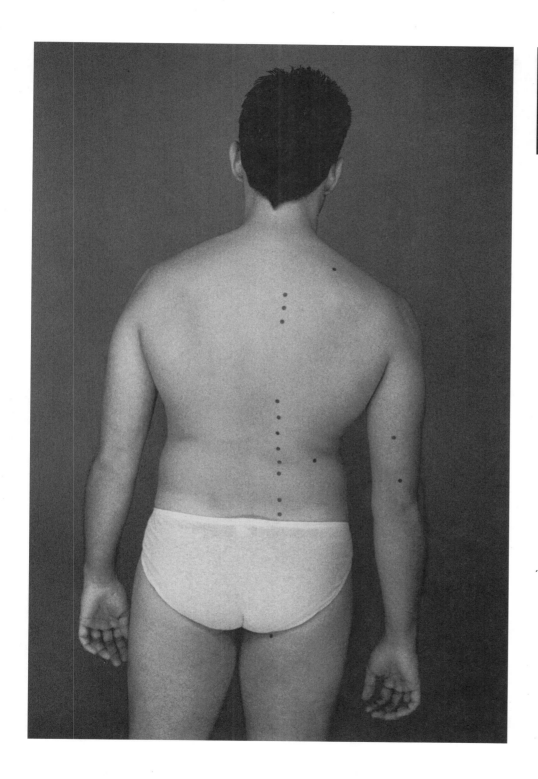

Pressure points of the back

TRIPLE WARMER # 15: TW-15

LOCATION: Superior to the scapula, in the center of the supraclavicular fossa. This point can be found level with the tip of the shoulder and midway towards the spine.
ANATOMY: The spinal accessory nerve and the supraclavicular nerve.
METHOD: Strike this point diagonally downward. It also will respond to thumb pressure.

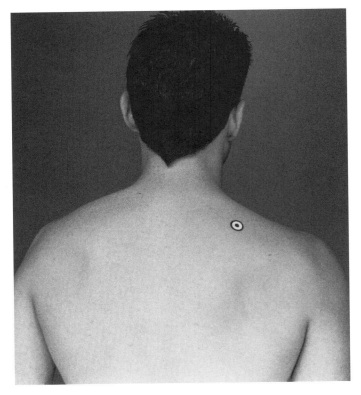

INTERSCAPULAR-PARASPINAL CLUSTER

Between the spine and the shoulder blades are three important points which control the circulatory and respiratory systems. These points can be attacked to produce serious consequences, [A] and are also very important for resuscitation [B] (see George A. Dillman Pressure Point Video Series # 5: Healing and Revival).

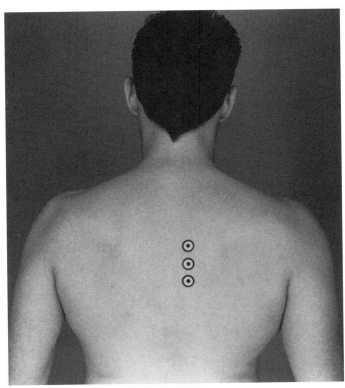

(Photo B: Jim Clapp, Newark, DE does revival to knock out victim)

BLADDER # 13: B-13

LOCATION: In the trapezius and rhomboid muscles, 1.5 AU lateral to the lower edge of the spinous process of the third thoracic vertebra (T-3). It is found between the shoulder-blade and the spine.
ANATOMY: A medial branch of the dorsal ramus of the third thoracic spinal nerve.
NOTE: This is the associated point of the lung meridian.

BLADDER # 14: B-14

LOCATION: In the trapezius and rhomboid muscles, 1.5 AU lateral to the lower edge of the spinous process of the fourth thoracic vertebra (T-4). It is found between the shoulder-blade and the spine, 1 AU below B-13.
ANATOMY: Directly on a medial cutaneous branch of the dorsal ramus of the fourth thoracic spinal nerve.
NOTE: This is the associated point of the pericardium meridian.

BLADDER # 15: B-15

LOCATION: In the trapezius and rhomboid muscles, 1.5 AU lateral to the lower edge of the spinous process of the fifth thoracic vertebra (T-5). It is found between the shoulder-blade and the spine, 1 AU below B-14.
ANATOMY: A medial branch of the dorsal ramus of the fifth thoracic spinal nerve.
NOTE: This is the associated point of the heart meridian.
METHOD: Strike these points from back to front.

WARNING: Because these points are related to the circulatory system, they should only be indicated during practice.

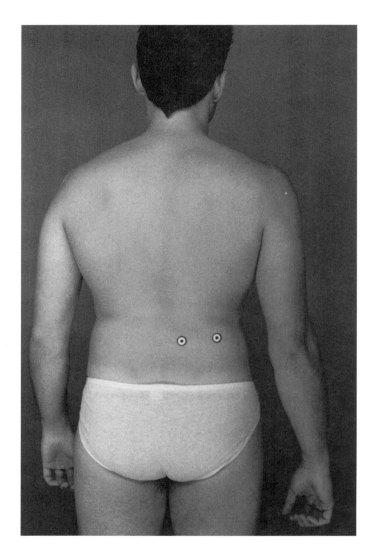

POSTERIOR KIDNEY POINT CLUSTER

BLADDER # 23: B-23

LOCATION: In the lumbodorsal fascia, between the longissimus and iliocostalis muscles, 1.5 AU lateral to the lower end of the spinous process of the 2nd lumbar vertebra (L-2). This point is beside the spine, level with the free end of the twelfth (floating) rib.
ANATOMY: Branches of the first lumbar spinal nerve.
NOTE: This point is the associated point of the kidney meridian.

GALL BLADDER # 25: GB-25

LOCATION: At the inferior border of the free end of the twelfth (floating) rib. This point is just at the tip of the smaller of the two floating ribs.
ANATOMY: The 11th intercostal nerve.
NOTE: GB-25 is the alarm point of the kidney meridian.
CAUTION: Do not strike these points.

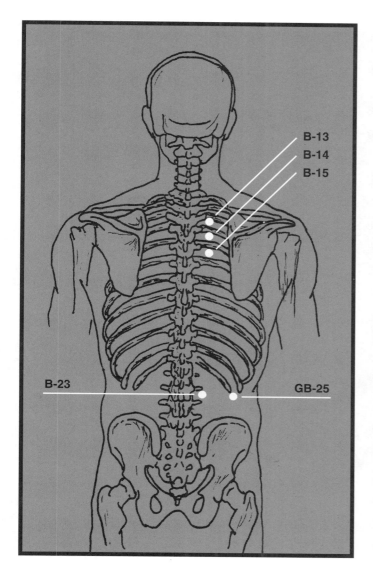

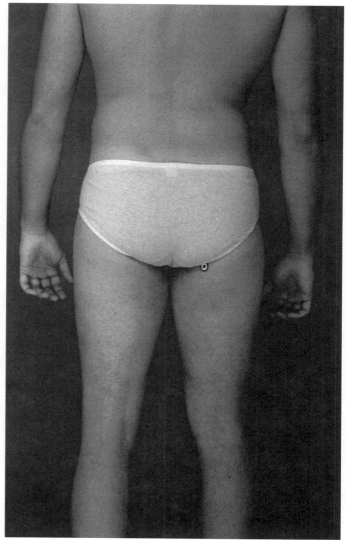

BLADDER # 50: B-50

LOCATION: At the inferior margin of the gluteus maximus muscle, at the midpoint of the transverse crease. This point can be found at the back of the thigh just below the buttocks.
ANATOMY: The posterior cutaneous nerve of the thigh and the sciatic nerve.
METHOD: Kick this point to immobilize the leg.

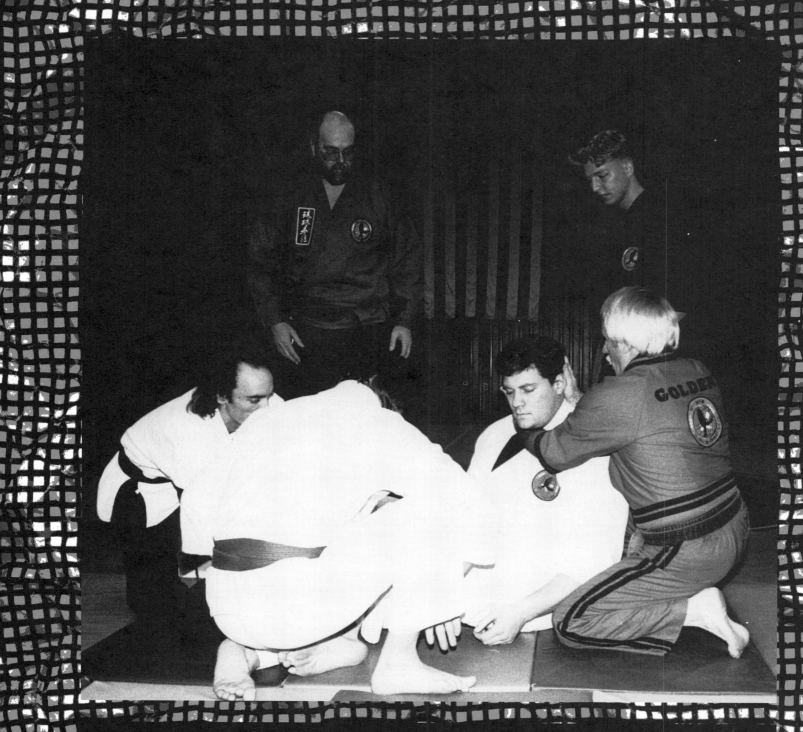

Bob Golden does revival on KO'd individual. (note: Others assist him, cross legs, etc.)

TUITE

Tuite (too-ee-tay, the Japanese pronunciation is torite, toe-ree-tay) refers to the grappling or joint manipulation aspect of Ryukyu kempo. However, joint manipulation cannot be separated out from the rest of Ryukyu kempo, as though it were a separate art. Tuite-waza (joint manipulation techniques) are performed in conjunction with kyusho-waza (pressure point techniques). In fact, tuite-waza qualify as kyusho-waza because pressure points are used to release the joints.

While tuite has much in common with Japanese jujitsu, it is not the same. Jujitsu (as it is usually taught and practiced) emphasizes joint-locking. The joint is turned or twisted to its maximum, then force is applied to cause pain-compliance, or injury. Tuite, on the other hand, stresses joint manipulation. Pressure points are used to cause a joint to release and relax, making it susceptible to injury. (Please note that this generalization does not characterize all styles of jujitsu. For example, Professor Wally Jay's Small Circle Theory jujitsu makes extensive use of acupoints in the application of techniques.)

Furthermore, in jujitsu, the joint control techniques are often the complete combative responses. However, in Ryukyu kempo, the tuite-waza do not exist independently of striking techniques. Hitting, kicking and joint control are part of a single response continuum, and only rarely is the joint attack the final technique. Most often, the tuite is followed by a decisive blow.

Nonetheless, the techniques of tuite can be used by themselves, either as a form of compassionate self-defense (using pain-compliance), or as the finishing technique. Kata contain many examples of techniques which are intended to break or dislocate joints. When applied mildly, many of these can be used to defeat an attacker without inflicting serious injury.

As we mentioned above, every kata movement has several interpretations and at least one of those is tuite. Even techniques which appear to be strikes, can be understood as joint manipulation. This means that understanding the principles of tuite is essential for proper interpretation of kata.

REVERSAL ACTION

The first, and simplest principle of tuite is the rule of reversal. The physiology of the body is such that, if a joint is resisting in one direction, it cannot withstand a sudden reversal of force. In other words, if you want to hyper-extend a joint, bend it first. As the opponent resists the bending action, he or she becomes immediately vulnerable to straightening and locking the joint. This can be demonstrated on any joint. For example, as a partner resists, bend his arm at the elbow, [A] then suddenly (but cautiously) change direction and straighten the arm. [B]

COMPLEX TORQUE

In much the same way as the inability of the body to resist sudden reversals of direction, it also cannot deal with complex torque. Complex torque means to manipulate a joint in more than one direction. Usually, this involves bending and twisting at the same time. The easiest example is a finger. If you grasp someone's finger and bend it straight back, there is usually pain. [A,B] However, if you grab and twist the finger, as you bend it, the pain is greatly intensified. [C] Applying complex torque makes the technique effective on virtually everyone, even those who are double jointed.

RELEASE POINTS

When thinking about pressure points, it is important to remember that each point has at least three functions. One of these is called "area control." This means that various points have a direct relationship on near-by joints. By manipulating these points, the corresponding joints become weakened. Attacking these points can be described as neuro-muscular manipulation.

These points cause the joint to release when properly stimulated. By "release" we mean that the muscles which work the joint, and guard it from injury, reflexively relax, leaving the joint essentially unprotected.

A good example of a release point is TW-11. TW-11, located one AU above the point of the elbow, works by stimulation of the Golgi's receptor. The Golgi's nerve bundle monitors the condition of the tendon which connects the triceps to the bone. When this point is stimulated by kneading, the muscles of the upper arm suddenly relax. Without resistance from the supporting musculature, the elbow is easily locked-out and damaged. [A,B]

This release is a body defense to protect the elbow by moving away from a perceived threat. Because this threat is not real, the arm instead becomes, at that moment, vulnerable to the application of a genuine elbow-lock as well as dislocation of the shoulder joint.

THREE BASIC TUITE TECHNIQUES

Since many tuite-waza are executed against the hand or arm, it is important to be familiar with three basic techniques common in kata application. Rather than approaching this from the point of view of technique (what I do to the opponent), we will look at the final position — or "shape" — of the opponent's limb when the tuite is applied. The exact manner in which the opponent's limb is manipulated into the desired position varies greatly among kata techniques. However, the end result is the same. By understanding clearly the end result, it is easier to understand the steps used to achieve it.

BASIC TUITE # 1: WRIST TURN AND PRESS

A. Rotate your partner's hand so that the little finger is up and the palm faces towards the outside of his body.

B. With your thumb, press upward on LI-4 in the web of the thumb, and with your fingers press down at SI-5 near the wrist driving your partner to the floor.

VARIATION:

C,D. With one hand, grasp your partner's hand in the little finger up position. With your other hand, press down at LI-11 near the elbow to drop your partner to the floor.

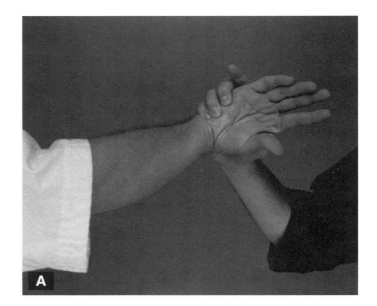

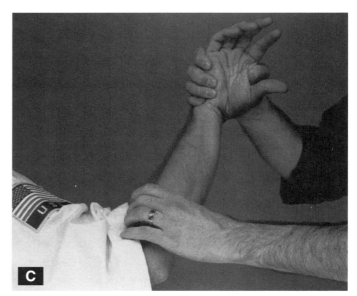

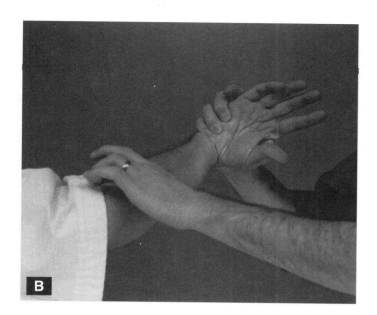

BASIC TUITE # 2: PALM TURN

A. Have your partner hold out a hand with the palm facing forward, the fingers pointed up and the elbow down. There should be about a 130 degree angle in your partner's wrist.

B. With one hand grab your partner's wrist and squeeze on the pressure points. With the other hand, grasp your partner's palm and press with your thumb against H-8 on the palm of his hand.

C. Rotate his palm, turning the little finger side back towards his centerline, while controlling his forearm with your other hand.

VARIATION:

D, E. Instead of concentrating on the point H-8, apply the technique by turning your partner's little finger behind his ring finger, then torque.

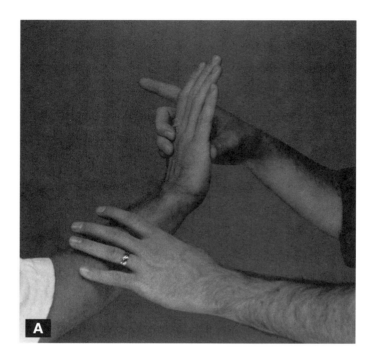

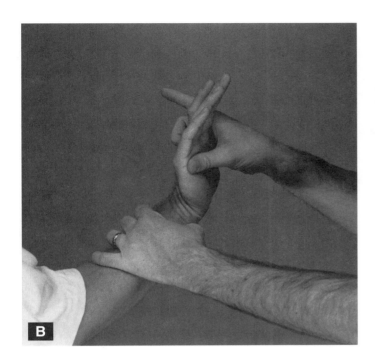

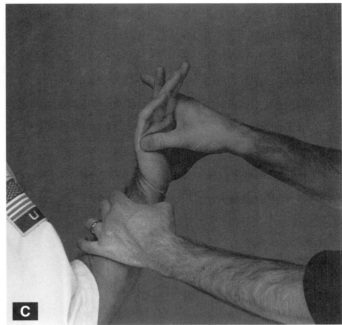

BASIC TUITE # 3: WRIST REVERSAL

A. Have your partner hold out one hand with the palm facing back. With one hand grasp his wrist on the pressure points, and with the other hand, wrap your fingers around the meat of his thumb, squeezing M-UE-13, while pressing against TW-3 on the back of his hand.

B. Rotate his hand, driving his little finger towards his rear outside diagonal.

C. Press his twisted arm diagonally to the rear to drive him to the ground.

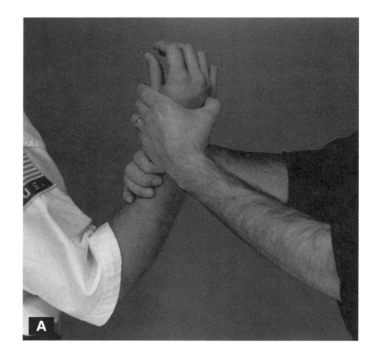

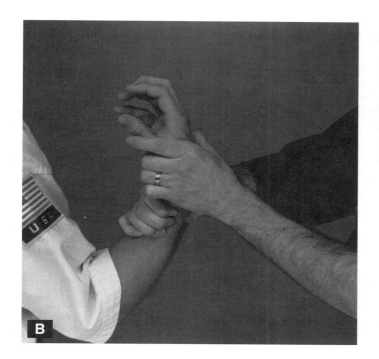

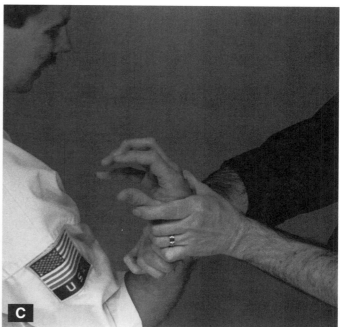

Barbara Converse (right) of Joliet, Illinois, applies a "chicken wing' thumb hold to her husband David.

George Dillman uses a kata move to demonstrate a knock out before a packed house seminar.

NAIHANCHI KATA

INTRODUCTION TO NAIHANCHI

There are three kata in the Naihanchi series which have a long history in karate. We will explain Naihanchi shodan, the first of the three. Virtually every style of karate, except goju-ryu and uechi-ryu, includes some version of one or more of them. In many older styles, Naihanchi kata are taught first. It is also well known that in ancient times great masters often only knew one single kata or one series of kata. If a master knew a kata series, more often than not it was Naihanchi.

The first Naihanchi kata has only 30 or so movements (the count can vary depending on how the sequences are broken down). There is only one stance — the straddle (or "horse") stance — and there is only side to side movement with a simple cross-over step. Because of the simplicity of the kata, a great deal of nonsense has been said about it. For example, there have been those who have said that this kata teaches fighting against a wall.

Supposedly, one is to back against a wall when faced with multiple attackers, to prevent them from circling around behind. In reality, being against a wall is the worst place to be, since it limits the defender's mobility far more than the attacker's.

Some have suggested that the kata movements are for fighting along the narrow walkways around rice paddies or for fighting on top of a wall, or for fighting in a narrow hallway. However, the movements of the kata cannot conceivably fit such interpretations. Furthermore, it is ludicrous to assume that the creator of Naihanchi would work so painstakingly to develop a form to fit so remote a contingency.

In addition to the ridiculous interpretations of Naihanchi which are given, students are often told, "Naihanchi is not a good kata for competition." And so, they complain about having to learn the form at all. In fact, no less than the late Masatoshi Nakayama wrote, "Since these [Naihanchi] kata are rather monotonous, turn the head briskly and strongly." What a thing to say! This kata is so boring you must turn your head briskly to stay awake. No wonder students find Naihanchi to be so pointless.

Gichin Funakoshi reported that the first ten years of his karate training consisted of only the three Naihanchi kata. If the misconceptions about Naihanchi were true in Funakoshi's day, then certainly its sole purpose must have been to test a student's perseverance and determination. "You must prove yourself by spending the next ten years washing the toilet and practicing Naihanchi. If you survive this test, we will teach you real karate."

However, the problem is not with the kata, it is with those who have taught the kata. The truth is that the three Naihanchi kata are so practical and effective that it takes ten years of study to exhaust their concepts and knowledge (actually, it takes a lifetime of study, but ten years is a good start.) Together, the three Naihanchi kata contain the secrets to 120 pressure points which can be used to quickly and effectively defeat an opponent.

This text will present secrets and insights into Naihanchi shodan which should astound any martial artist with the wisdom to recognize what we are revealing. Nonetheless, we are still only scratching the surface. There is far more to learn than we can possibly include. But, more important than the interpretation of the kata presented here, are the principles which are applied. These principles are keys to unlocking the hidden meanings of any traditional form.

SEQUENCE OF NAIHANCHI KATA

Note: Most descriptions of this kata use what we now know are misleading terms to describe the techniques (such as "Haishu-uke: block with the back of the hand"). Instead, we will describe these movements using neutral language — terms such as thrust, sweep, whip, in place of words like punch, block, strike which suggest a particular interpretation.

OPENING

1. Stand with heels together and the toes turned out slightly, hands at the sides.

2. Bow respectfully, keeping the eyes forward.

TECHNIQUE # 1

1. Bring both hands up, placing the back of the right open hand against the left palm, at about chin level.
2. Draw the hands in towards the solar plexus.
3. Turn the fingers towards the floor, and press the hands forward and down. At the same time, draw the feet together, so that they touch heel and ball, pointing straight forward, and bend the knees very slightly.

TECHNIQUE # 2

4. Step the left foot towards the right, crossing in front of the right leg. The hips will naturally turn slightly towards the right.

TECHNIQUE # 3

1. Draw the right foot from behind the left stepping out into a straddle stance and sharply whip the open right hand directly to the right side, palm facing forward. At the same time, draw the left hand into a tight fist at the left hip.

TECHNIQUE # 4

2. Smartly smack the left elbow into the right palm towards the right side.

TECHNIQUE # 5

3. In a sharp movement, bring both fists to the right hip, left above right, palms facing each other, while turning the head to look to the left.

TECHNIQUE # 6

4. Sweep the left fist to the left side, about level with the middle of the thigh.

TECHNIQUE # 7

1. In a short hooking motion, thrust the right fist to the left, while drawing the left fist to the left hip.

2. Without changing the position of the hands, cross-step to the left with the right foot.

TECHNIQUE # 8

1. Look to the front, while stepping out with the left foot into a straddle stance.
2. Sweep the right fist up and forward, ending palm facing back, even with the right shoulder.

TECHNIQUE # 9

1. Bring the left fist forward and down.
2. Draw the right and left arms across the centerline of the body.
3. Sweep the left fist up and forward, and the right fist down and forward.

TECHNIQUE # 10

1. Bring the right fist, palm down, under the left elbow and thrust the left fist up and out at head height.
2. Snap the left arm back to its initial position.

TECHNIQUE # 11

3. Draw the left knee up, sweeping the left foot towards the right knee, until the toes touch the inside of the right leg.

TECHNIQUE # 12

4. Step back down into straddle stance. Turning the fist over sharply sweep the left hand to the left front diagonal while maintaining the position of the right hand at the left elbow.

TECHNIQUE # 13

1. Draw the right knee up, sweeping the right foot towards the left knee, until the toes touch the inside of the left leg.

TECHNIQUE # 14

2. Set the right foot back down, resuming the straddle stance. Sweep the left hand to the right diagonal, turning the fist sharply back to a palm up position, and maintaining the right hand at the left elbow.

TECHNIQUE # 15

3. Bring the fists quickly to the right hip, left over right, palms facing each other, and look to the left side.

TECHNIQUE # 16

4. Thrust both fists towards the left side, the right fist moving in a short hooking motion and stopping even with the edge of the torso, the left fist stretching out fully to the left side.

TECHNIQUE # 17

1. Open the left hand, and with a slight circling motion, turn it so the palm faces forward. At the same time, draw the right fist to the right hip.

TECHNIQUE # 18

2. Smartly smack the right elbow into the left palm towards the left side.

TECHNIQUE # 19

3. In a sharp movement, bring both fists to the left hip, right above left, palms facing each other, while turning the head to look to the right.

TECHNIQUE # 20

4. Sweep the right fist to the right side, about level with the middle of the thigh.

TECHNIQUE # 21

1. In a short hooking motion, thrust the left fist to the right, while drawing the right fist to the right hip.
2. Without changing the position of the hands, cross-step to the right with the left foot.

TECHNIQUE # 22

1. Look to the front, while stepping out with the right foot into a straddle stance, sweeping the left fist up and forward. This movement ends with the palm facing back, level with the left shoulder.

TECHNIQUE # 23

1. Bring the right fist forward and down.
2. Draw the left and right arms across the centerline of the body.
3. Sweep the right fist up and forward, and the left fist down and forward.

TECHNIQUE # 24

1. Bring the left fist, palm down, under the right elbow and thrust the right fist up and out at head height.
 2. Snap the right arm back to its initial position.

TECHNIQUE # 25

3. Draw the right knee up, sweeping the right foot towards the left knee, until the toes touch the inside of the left leg.

TECHNIQUE # 26

4. Step back down into straddle stance. Turning the fist over sharply, sweep the right hand to the right front diagonal while maintaining the position of the left hand at the right elbow.

TECHNIQUE # 27

1. Draw the left knee up, sweeping the left foot towards the right knee, until the toes touch the inside of the right leg.

TECHNIQUE # 28

2. Set the left foot back down, resuming the straddle stance. Sweep the right hand to the left diagonal, turning the fist sharply back to a palm up position, maintaining the left hand at the right elbow.

TECHNIQUE # 29

3. Bring the fists quickly to the left hip, right over left, palms facing each other, and look to the right side.

TECHNIQUE # 30

4. With a strong kiai (shout) thrust both fists towards the right side, the left fist moving in a short hooking motion and stopping even with the edge of the torso, the right fist stretching out fully to the right side.

TECHNIQUE # 31

1. Draw the right foot up to the left and stand upright. Bring both hands up, placing the back of the right hand against the left palm, at about chin level.
2. Draw the hands in towards the solar plexus.
3. Turn the hands down, and press them forward and down in front of the belt.

TECHNIQUE # 32

1. Draw the hands into fists at the hips.
2. Step to the right with the right foot, into a natural shoulder-width position.
3. Thrust both fists down and forward.

CLOSING

4. Bring the feet together and the hands to the sides in a posture of attention.
5. Bow respectfully, keeping the eyes forward.

NAIHANCHI KATA

| Opening A | Opening B | 1 a | 1 b | 1 c |

| 8 a | 8 b | 9 a | 9 b | 9 c | 10 a |

| 17 | 18 | 19 | 20 | 21 a | 21 b |

| 26 | 27 | 28 | 29 | 30 | 31 a |

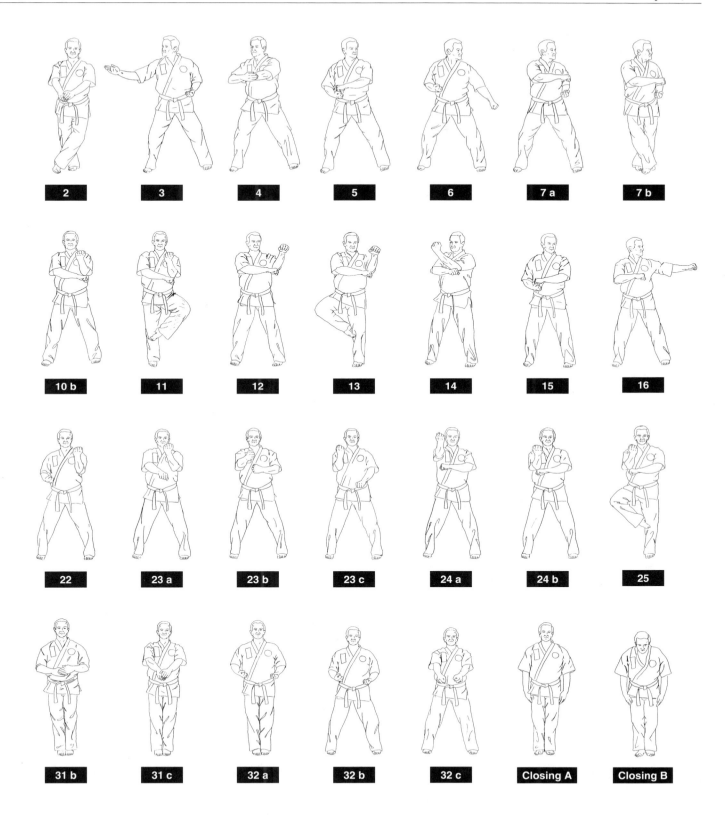

Ed Lake of Lantana, FL demonstrates a knockout with the closing move of kata Nai Hanchi, page 179 (3).

BUNKAI

COMMON INCORRECT APPLICATIONS

For readers to fully appreciate the effectiveness and reasonableness of Ryukyu kempo interpretations of this kata, it is first necessary to understand the ineffective explanations given by most karate instructors. What follows is the common bunkai as given in various books, and/or generally taught in most dojos. It should be noted that this is representative of what most karate students learn with respect to this kata. What any particular karate school teaches may differ somewhat from what we show here.

1. After performing the bow and technique # 1 as an opening salutation, stand with feet together and hands in front of your groin as an attacker approaches from the left.

2. Cross step towards the right, to get closer to the attacker.

3. As the attacker punches, step into the punch and block with the back of the right hand. (Step into the attack and block? This will not work unless the attacker is punching the air. If the punch is directed against you, you must step away from it to block. And, what about the left hand, what is it doing?)

4. Pull your attacker into an elbow strike. (This interpretation does not fit the steps of the kata. To reach with the elbow requires either an extra movement, or a gross leaning of the body [A]. Some suggest that the object is to pull the attacker's head into your elbow [B]. However, this won't work. If you block a punch, then try to pull the attacker into an elbow strike, you will find that he can easily resist your efforts while punching you at will.)

5. Turn your head to look at your attacker on the left, while drawing your hands to your right hip. (Why hide your hands at your hips? Who fights that way?)

6. As your opponent attacks your left side with a thrust kick, block with your left arm. (If your opponent is kicking in earnest you will not be able to stop the kick. Instead, his kick will smash through the attempted block, possibly breaking the small ulnar bone of the arm in the process.)

7. As your attacker steps forward after the kick is blocked, punch him with your right hand. (The movement, as practiced in the kata, won't reach the attacker, because it stops at the edge of the body.) [A]. Furthermore, if the kick was successfully blocked, won't the attacker simply continue with punches?

8a & 8b. Your next opponent is not directly in front of you, but rather, off to the left, so you step with your right leg in a cross-over step.

9. Step to the side with your left foot (straddling the body of your previous adversary?) to stand directly in front of your opponent and block with your right arm as he attacks with a left punch (even though your groin is completely exposed to a kick).

10. Your opponent presses the attack by punching to your head with his right hand while simultaneously punching to your body with his left. You block both techniques with a left high block and a right low block.

11. Your opponent attempts one more left punch, which you deflect with your right hand, while punching him in the face with your left hand. (The opponent has been allowed to attack without response until the fourth punch.)

12. You are surrounded by three opponents, one to the left side, one on each of the forward diagonals.

13. The assailant on the left diagonal attacks first with a kick which you block using a left crescent kick.

14. The attacker continues his assault with a left punch which you block with your left hand, keeping your right hand under your elbow. (You then stop worrying about him, because somehow, he has lost interest in fighting and stopped his aggression, making it unnecessary for you to counter-attack.)

15. The attacker on the right diagonal attacks with a foot sweep.

16. Avoid the sweep by lifting your right leg.

17. The attacker continues his assault with a punch which you block with your left hand, while your right fist remains under your elbow. (This attacker also is suddenly overcome by an urge to stop attacking.)

18. You bring your fists to your right hip and look at the attacker to your left.

19. As the attacker attempts to punch, you quickly intercept him, stopping him mid-attack with a double punch, striking him head and body. (This might work, but, it doesn't look anything like the move in the kata, the final positions are completely different. [A])

Sandra Schlessman, George Dillman, Jerry Stephenson demonstrate knockouts.

RYUKYU KEMPO BUNKAI

The common karate explanation just given, contained numerous blocks, several movements without meanings and only six offensive techniques in the whole kata. If this is what kata means then it is no wonder people consider it useless.

In contrast, the explanations given here for Ryukyu kempo are real applications that work. It must be remembered that we are only scratching the surface of what the kata contains.

In explaining the kata, we will break down the techniques individually. We will demonstrate how steps can work together in the exact sequence of the kata. **It is our firm belief that kata movements are to be interpreted as self-defense techniques in the precise order in which they appear in the kata.** Some individuals say that kata movements done out of order or backwards, are the correct bunkai for some self-defense. This is ludicrous for no ancient master would have practiced his movements this way. Remember, kata was developed to enable the originator to visualize and perform tuite and kyusho attacks with precision—and according to the diurnal and destructive cycles of Eastern medicine. You don't find sports teams of any nation practicing their plays backwards.

Each application has a number which refers to the technique in the kata. Since Naihanchi is a symmetrical form, each movement occurs on the right and left side, and this is reflected in the numbering system. # 16/30 is the double thrust technique which ends each segment. # 16 is the performance on the left side and # 30 is to the right. Though the bunkai are demonstrated only one time each, the reader should understand that if, for example, # 16 is used against a right handed attack, then # 30 would be for a left handed assault.

RYUKYU KEMPO BUNKAI

TECHNIQUES # 1, 2 & 3

At a basic level these two techniques are combined together, though other applications interpret them separately. Remember, these actions were interpreted only as a salutation and a preparatory movement in karate, followed by a step and block.

1. An attacker moves to push you with his right hand.
2. Bring both your hands over his hand, trapping it against your chest.
3. With the fingers of your right hand, lift your opponent's little finger and draw it behind his ring finger.
4. Press the edge of your left wrist against pressure point SI-6 on the attacker's wrist.

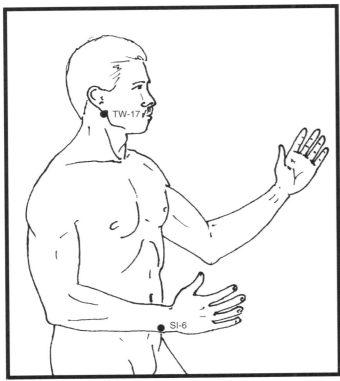

TECHNIQUES # 1, 2 & 3 *(continued)*

5. Perform the cross-over step (technique # 2), allowing your body to turn naturally toward the right.

Your opponent is now caught in a basic tuite technique, the palm twist described in chapter four.
6. Step to the right into a straddle stance, while applying pressure on the opponent's hand.
7&8. As the opponent moves to release pressure on his wrist by stepping to your right, strike against TW-17 below the ear with a right back-hand strike. (This corresponds to technique # 3 of the kata).
NOTE: See natural motion of this move on page 150.

TECHNIQUES # 1, 2 & 3 *(continued)*

The back-hand is not perfectly flat, but is cupped slightly so that the knuckles protrude [A]. As the strike is delivered the knuckles fit into the cavity behind the jaw where TW-17 is situated [B & C].

TECHNIQUE # 3/17

This technique was interpreted as a block in the karate explanation.

1. Your opponent attempts a right punch.
2. Intercept his attack and grab his wrist firmly on the pressure points (H-6 & L-8, or L-7 & SI-6, depending on how you catch his fist).
3. Pull his captured right hand strongly to your hip, and step towards him into a straddle stance.
4. Strike TW-17 with the back of your open right hand.

As you strike you may adjust your target depending on the distance, angle and size of your opponent. If he is somewhat larger than you, and your full reach is needed to strike his head, then attack TW-17, under his ear.

If your attacker is somewhat smaller than you, or your strong action of pulling his right arm draws his head in close, then strike him at the base of the skull on GB-20, using your forearm as a weapon. [A].

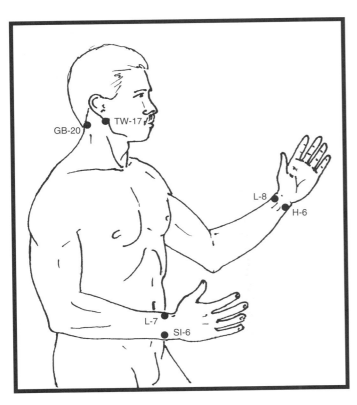

TECHNIQUE # 4/18

The karate application was to pull the attacker into an elbow strike. This Ryukyu kempo application is a devastating example of tuite.

1. Your opponent reaches to grab you with his right hand.
2. Give him your left arm to grab onto.
3. Grasp his right wrist with your right hand, squeezing pressure points H-6 and L-8, and trap his hand to your arm.

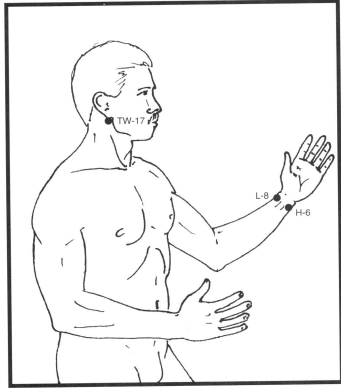

TECHNIQUE # 4/18 *(continued)*

4. Rotate your left elbow forward, turning his right hand in an example of the tuite palm twist.

5 & 6. Using the palm twist for control, bring your opponent's head into your elbow, striking below the ear to TW-17.

TECHNIQUE # 5/19, 6/20

In the karate interpretation technique # 5/19 (hands at hips) had no meaning. In Ryukyu kempo stacked hands always means a joint manipulation technique.

1. Your opponent grabs your lapel with his right hand.
2. Reach your right hand over his, and grasp him firmly on wrist points H-6 and L-8.
3 & 4. Using your left hand for additional support, twist his hand off of your lapel.
5 & 6. Step back with your right leg into a straddle stance, sideways to your opponent, while drawing his right hand to your hip.

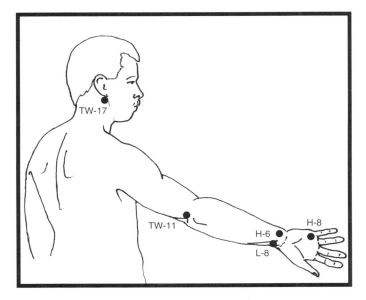

TECHNIQUE # 5/19, 6/20 *(continued)*

7a. Roll your left elbow onto the back of your opponent's arm, and press down on TW-11 in the triceps tendon.

8. Slip your right hand up against the back of his captured hand, and squeeze with your fingers on H-8 in the palm of his hand, while twisting to keep his little finger down.

9 & 10. Sweeping the left fist outward, strike your opponent under the ear at TW-17.

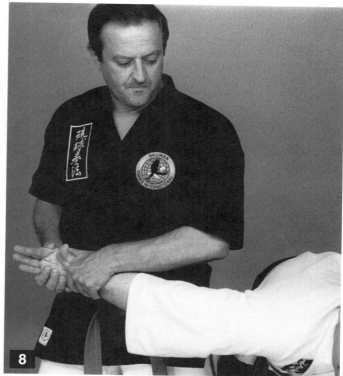

TECHNIQUE # 6/20

The karate explanation for this was to block a kick.

1. Your opponent grasps your right wrist with his left hand.

2. Circle your right wrist to the outside to turn his left arm over, while stepping back with your right leg, pulling and stretching his left arm.

3 & 4. Strike down with your left hand against the middle of his triceps, at point TW-12, to drop him to the floor.

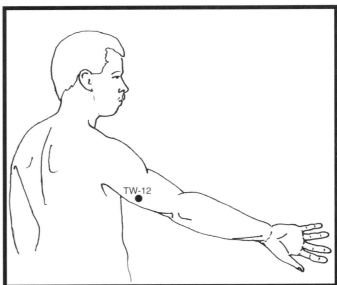

TECHNIQUE # 6/20 (Second Application)

1. Your opponent grabs your right wrist with his right hand.

2. Draw your right hand in and up, turning his right arm over and grasping his wrist on points SI-6 and L-7.

3. Step back with your right leg into a straddle stance sideways to your opponent, while pulling and stretching his right arm. Press the knuckles of your left fist against the Golgi's tendon receptor, pressure point TW-11, just above the point of your opponent's elbow.

4. Knead this point to release the elbow and drive the attacker to the floor.

These are examples of the use of pressure points to release a joint and make it vulnerable to attack.

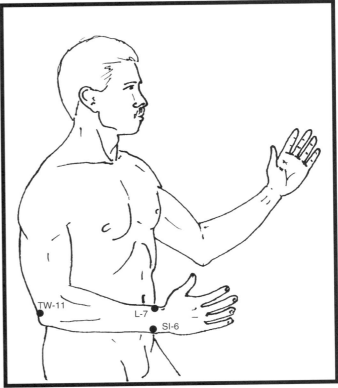

TECHNIQUE # 7/21 (A)

The karate interpretation was a short punch.

1. Your opponent attacks with a left punch.

2 & 3. Deflect and grab his left wrist from the outside with your left hand, squeezing on the wrist pressure points L-8 and H-6.

The deflect and grab is covered in APPENDIX B: How to Catch a Punch, in **KYUSHO-JITSU: The Dillman Method of Pressure Point Fighting** (259-265).

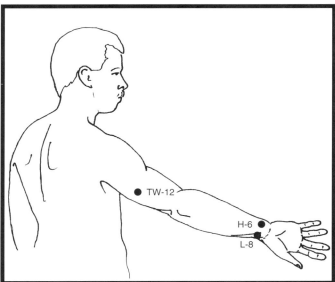

TECHNIQUE # 7/21 (A) *(continued)*

4. Pull the attacker's left palm against your left hip.

5, 6. Punch with your right hand in the middle of his triceps at TW-12.

TECHNIQUE # 7/21 (B)

1. You have struck the opponent's triceps and knocked him off balance, as in the previous technique.

2 & 3. Using the crossover step from the kata, kick your opponent on point N-LE-7, outside and below the knee to release the leg.

4. As the opponent's leg buckles, press behind his knee with your left foot.

5. Stomp down strongly, driving your opponent's knee to the floor.

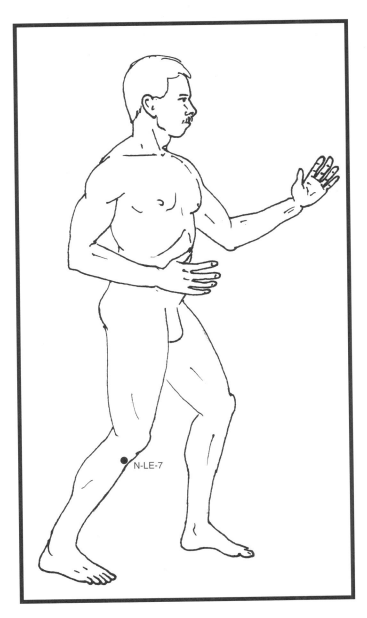

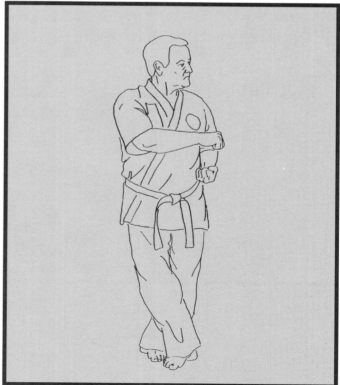

TECHNIQUE # 7/21, 8/22

1. As your attacker attempts a left punch, capture his wrist and pull it to your left hip as before.

2. With the knuckles of your right hand, knead TW-11, the Golgi's receptor point, just above his elbow.

3. As his shoulder releases, maintain pressure on him by walking to the left, using a crossover stance.

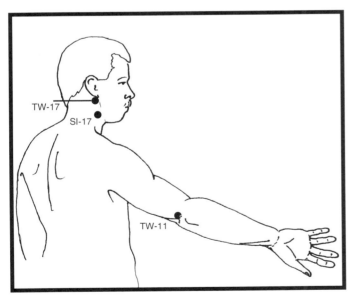

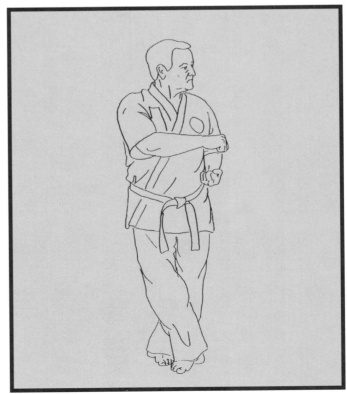

TECHNIQUE # 7/21, 8/22 *(continued)*

4. Continue by stepping out with your left leg into a straddle stance.

This technique works well for driving someone into a wall or other obstacle.

5. To continue with kata technique # 8/22, release the pressure on his elbow with your right fist, but continue holding his hand against your left side.

6. As your opponent lifts his head, strike with your right fist against TW-17, or SI-17.

TECHNIQUE # 8/22

In karate this technique is a simple block.

1. Your opponent attacks with a left punch.

2 & 3. Deflect and grasp his left wrist on points H-6 and L-8 with your left hand and pull it strongly to your hip.

4 & 5. Strike with your right fist under his ear at TW-17, or at the base of the skull at GB-20 (depending on how far his head turns).

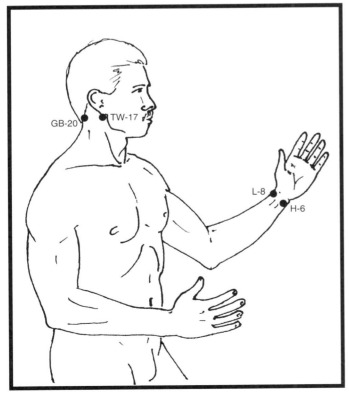

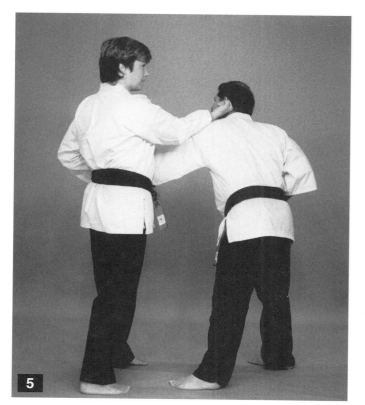

TECHNIQUE # 9/23

The karate explanation was double blocking.

1. The opponent grabs your lapel with his right hand, and threatens with his left.

2 & 3. With your right hand, punch the attacker in the crease of his hip, about 2" to the side of his groin, hitting Sp-12 & Li-12 (inguinal crease cluster).

Striking Sp-12 & Li-12 will cause your opponent to bend forward, with his face up (almost the same position as bowing before a kata). This action stretches out the nerves in the neck.

4 & 5. With your left fist, strike upward, just inside the notch on the bottom of the jaw, hitting S-5.

In this application, the double technique which is performed as a simultaneous movement in the kata, is executed with a slightly broken timing, allowing one fist to strike an instant before the other. This technique utilizes two principles of kyusho-jitsu, the cycle of destruction (liver/wood & spleen/earth) and the principle of yin and yang (spleen/yin to stomach/yang).

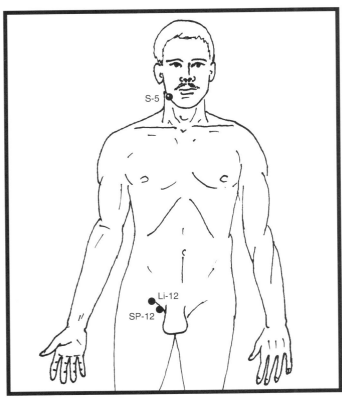

TECHNIQUE # 10/24

1. Your opponent grabs your lapel with his right hand, while threatening to punch with his left.

2. With your right hand grasp his wrist points L-7 and SI-6.

3 & 4. Strike down on his forearm with the point of your elbow, on point L-5.

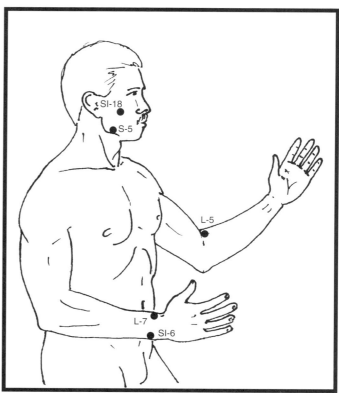

TECHNIQUE # 10/24 *(continued)*

As you strike down on his arm with your elbow, the crossed-extensor reflex will cause his left shoulder to move back away from you, so that he is unable to carry out his threat to punch.

5 & 6. As his head jerks down and forward, strike immediately upwards, under the jaw at S-5 or under the cheekbone at SI-18.

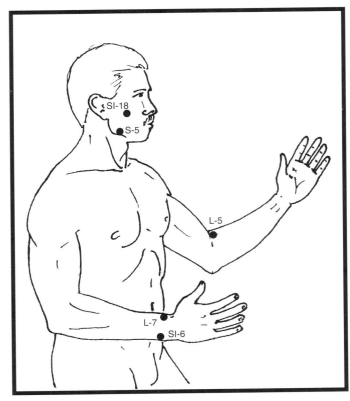

TECHNIQUE # 11/13/25/27

In the karate application the foot movement is interpreted as blocking or avoiding a sweep.

1. An opponent faces you in a threatening posture.

2 - 5. Preempt his attack by kicking against Sp-9, inside and below the knee, to drive him to the ground.

It is difficult to see a kick within this movement, which is bringing your foot up by your own knee. However, what the kata does is map out the pressure points you are to attack, by placing your foot on those pressure points on your own leg. Your heel touches Sp-10 and your toes touch Sp-9 [A].

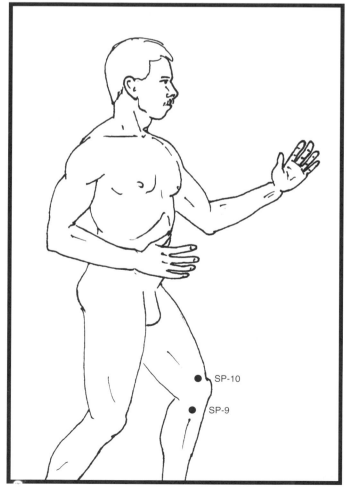

SP-10

SP-9

TECHNIQUE # 12/26

In the karate application, this move was blocking.

1 & 2. Your opponent attacks with a right punch.

3. Evade the attack by moving to your left, and positioning yourself on the diagonal to your opponent. At the same time, catch his forearm with your left hand, grasping firmly on L-5.

4 & 5. Strike with the little finger side of your right fist, hooking behind the attacker's jaw to catch TW-17.

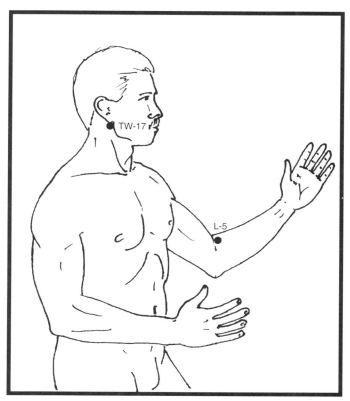

TECHNIQUE # 11/25 & 12/26

1. Your opponent punches with his right arm.

2 - 6. Simultaneously, strike down on point LI-7 in the middle of his forearm with your left fist, kick Sp-10 inside and above his left knee with your right foot, and strike TW-17 under his right ear with your right fist, knocking him to the ground.

In this application, you combine in one motion the footwork of technique #11/25 and the handwork of #12/26.

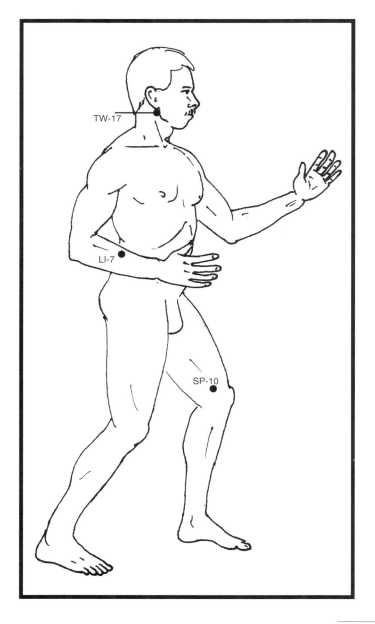

TECHNIQUE # 11/25 & 12/26 (continued)

TECHNIQUE # 14/28

In the karate application, this move was blocking.

1. Your opponent grabs your lapel with his left hand while threatening to punch with his right.

2. With your left hand grasp his left arm near the elbow, digging with your fingertips into pressure points LI-10 and H-3.

3. Strike with the little finger side of your right fist, hooking behind the attacker's jaw to catch TW-17.

4. Follow through with the right hand, performing the movement just as in the kata.

5. Maintain your grip on the opponent's arm, because even a very light blow (as used during filming) will stagger him. This enables you to keep control for a follow-up attack if necessary.

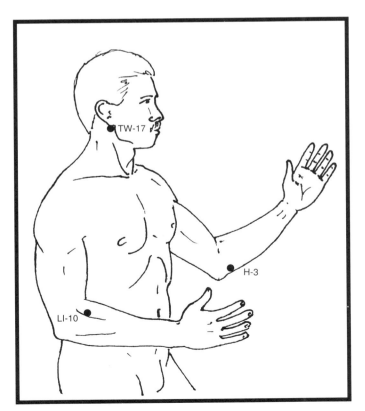

TECHNIQUE # 15/29, 16/30

Hands at the hip (#15/29) had no meaning in the karate interpretation.

1. Your opponent reaches out with his right hand either to push, or to grab.

2-3. Catch his fingers with your left hand (thumb-side down).

4. Raise his right hand up slightly (to create a reversal of direction), and place your right hand on the little finger side of his wrist, pressing on SI-6.

5 & 6. Cut across SI-6 and pull your right hand back while pressing and rotating against the little finger side of his palm (this is the basic tuite palm twist).

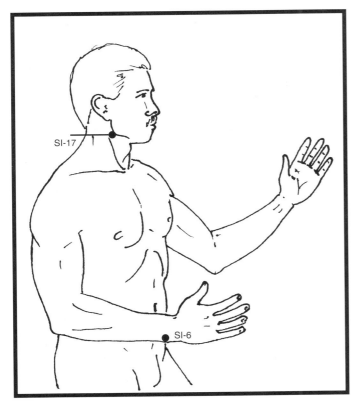

TECHNIQUE # 15/29, 16/30 *(continued)*

7. Pull your hands sharply towards your right hip and secure a firm grip on his wrist with your right hand. At the same time, step to the right into a straddle stance.

8-9. Holding his arm outstretched with your right hand, strike with your left fist against SI-17 at the bend of the jaw.

TECHNIQUE # 3/17 & 16/30

Techniques # 3/17 and 16/30 frame the kata, one at the beginning and the other at the end of the kata segments. This means that these two techniques are intended to work with any of the other techniques. If for any reason a technique is not working properly, return to # 3/17 or # 16/30. Typically, the back hand technique is used on the inside line (meaning that you are positioned directly in front of your opponent, between his hands) [A]. Similarly, the double thrust is usually used from the outside line (meaning you are positioned slightly to the side of your opponent, away from his opposite arm) [B]. The following sequence illustrates how easily they can be utilized.

TECHNIQUES # 5/19, 3/17, & 16/30

1. Your opponent seizes you by the lapel with his left hand, while threatening a right punch.

2-3. You grasp his wrist with both hands and attempt to twist his arm away.

At this point, your attempt to perform technique # 5 fails: perhaps you have missed the pressure points, or, perhaps your opponent is resistant at the wrist points.

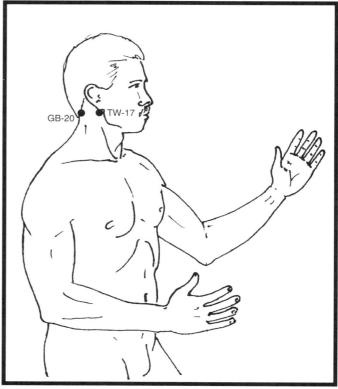

TECHNIQUES # 5/19, 3/17, & 16/30 *(continued)*

4. Do not struggle to complete the joint lock, simply clamp down strongly with your right hand, and pull his left hand towards your right hip (do not be concerned if his hand comes off your lapel, or moves at all to your hip).

5-6. At the same time strike your opponent's head under the ear at TW-17 or at the hollow of the neck at GB-20 using the back of your open left hand.

7-8. Immediately turn your left hand over and firmly grasp the attacker's left ear, using it to drive him to the ground.

ADDITIONAL APPLICATIONS AND VARIATIONS

VARIATION ON # 1/31

1. Your opponent grabs you by the lapel with both hands, pulling you in.

2. Bring both your arms up, cutting across LI-7 on the outside of his forearms to press his elbows in towards his centerline.

3-4. Press or poke upward with the tips of your fingers on SI-17, behind the point of the jaw.

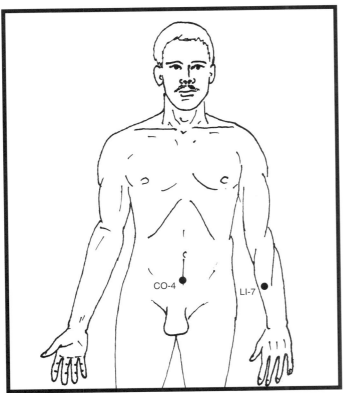

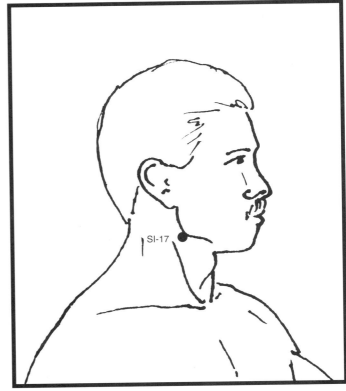

VARIATION ON # 1/31 *(continued)*

5-7. Bring your hands downward, and press them strongly into Co-4 (tanden point cluster), just behind the knot of his belt.

Co-4 is the alarm point of the small intestine meridian.

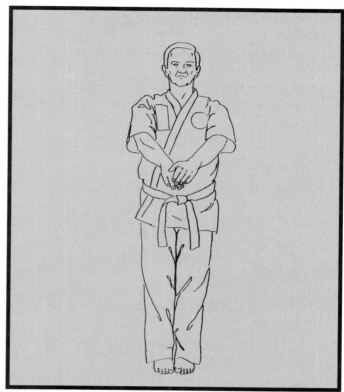

VARIATION ON # 7/21(A) & 8/22

1. Your opponent grabs you with his left hand, and pulls you forward, threatening a right punch.

2. With your left hand grasp his wrist points L-7 and SI-6.

3-4. Using your right hand, punch the side of his biceps at point LI-13 while stepping to the left into a straddle stance.

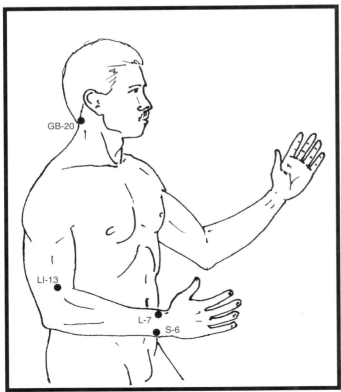

VARIATION ON # 7/21(A) & 8/22 *(continued)*

5-8. Strike upwards with your right fist into the base of his skull at GB-20.

Note the use of a single-knuckle fist.

COMBINING # 5/19, 11/13

1. Your opponent grabs your lapel with his right hand.

2. Reach your right hand over his, and grasp him firmly on wrist points H-6 and L-8.

3. Using your left hand for additional support, you attempt to twist his hand off of your lapel and down to your hip.

At this point, your attempt to perform technique # 5/19 fails: perhaps you have missed the pressure points, or, perhaps your opponent is resistant at the wrist points.

4-5. As your opponent resists your efforts, execute technique # 11/13, kicking SP-10 inside his left knee.

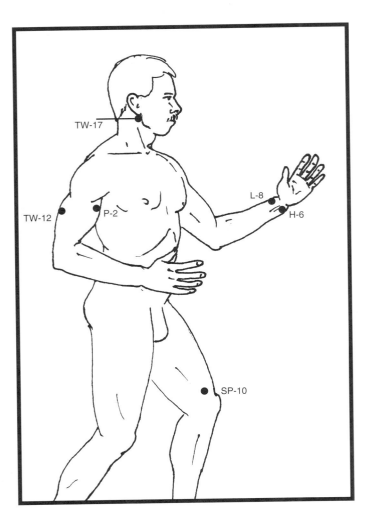

COMBINING # 5/19, 11/13 *(continued)*

6-8. Step back from the kick with your right leg into a straddle stance sideways to your opponent while drawing his right hand to your hip.

9. Pressing with your left elbow on TW-12 in the middle of his triceps, pin his arm against the top of your left leg, so that the point P-2 is pressed against your thigh.

10. The opponent can be finished off with a strike to the head at TW-17, under the ear.

VARIATION ON # 16/30

1. You face an opponent who is ready to attack.

2-3. As he punches with a straight left, move outside of his punch, slipping your right foot behind his left and perform a "two-hand catch" to capture his left hand on pressure points H-6 and L-8 (See APPENDIX B: How to Catch a Punch, in *KYUSHO-JITSU: The Dillman Method of Pressure Point Fighting*, 259-265).

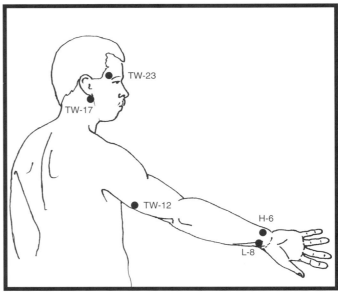

VARIATION ON # 16/30 *(continued)*

4-5. Strike across TW-12 in the middle of his upper arm using the bony prominence of your right wrist.

6. In a continuous movement, attack TW-17 under the ear.

7. An alternative is to attack TW-23, the terminus point of the Triple Warmer meridian, while pressing with your knee against his captured left leg.

VARIATION ON # 16/30

1. Your opponent reaches to grab or push you with both hands.

2-3. Deflect his right hand towards the left, as you slide your right arm outside his arm.

4. Seize his right arm with your right hand, grasping on the wrist points H-6 and L-8.

5. Grasp his hair with your left hand, activating the bladder points on the scalp.

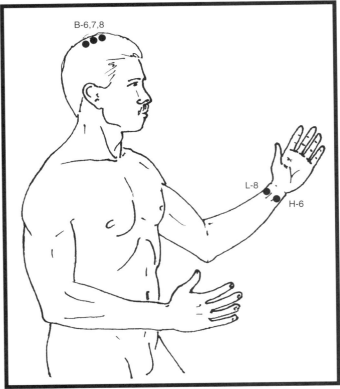

VARIATION ON # 16/30 *(continued)*

6-9. With a circular motion manipulate your opponent's head to control him at will.

This technique works best on an opponent with thick and fairly long hair. Grasp him firmly so that the foreknuckles of your fist rub on the scalp points.

VARIATION ON # 16/30 *(continued)*

If your opponent is thinning or bald on top, grab the side or back of the head to activate the points there. If your opponent is completely bald, or has a very short haircut, grab the ear firmly. [A] (Remember, acupuncturists have long known that the ear is a complete pressure point microcosm for the whole body, and have long practiced auricular acupuncture.)

An important point in this application is the use of a circular motion. The best way to understand this is to grab a training partner by the hair and ask him to resist as you pull forward. Though he will experience some pain, he can do it. [B] Then, pull his head in a small circle, and he will not be able to resist. [C,D,E] This is an example of the principle of complex torque. Since it is impossible to resist in more than one direction at a time, the circle causes complete vulnerability in any direction.

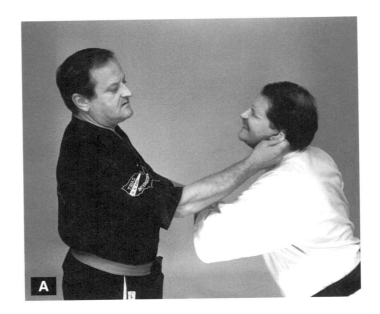

SELECTED BIBLIOGRAPHY & SOURCES

ACADEMY OF TRADITIONAL
CHINESE MEDICINE
An Outline of Chinese Acupuncture
Chan's Corporation
Monterey Park, CA, 1983

BEIJING COLLEGE OF TRADITIONAL
CHINESE MEDICINE et. al
Essentials of Chinese Acupuncture
Pergamon Press LTD
Elmsford, New York, 1981

DILLMAN, George A.
Pressure Point Video Instructional Series
Dillman Karate International
Reading, PA

DILLMAN, George A. with THOMAS, Chris
**Kyusho-Jitsu: The Dillman Method of
Pressure Point Fighting**
Dillman Karate International
Reading, PA, 1992

EGAMI, Shigeru
The Heart of Karate-Do
Kodansha International
Tokyo, 1980

ELLIS, Andrew, WISEMAN, Nigel, BOSS, Ken
Fundamentals of Chinese Acupuncture
Paradigm Publications
Brookline, Mass., 1988

FUNAKOSHI, Gichin
Ryukyu Kempo: Karate 1922

Karate-Do Kyohan
tr. T. Ohshima
Kodansha International
Tokyo, 1973

Karate-Do Nyumon
Kodansha International
Tokyo, 1988

GUYTON, Arthur C., M.D.
Text Book of Medical Physiology, 7th ed.
W. B. Saunders, Co.
Philadelphia, 1986

HISATAKA, Masayuki
Scientific Karate-Do
Japan Publications
Tokyo, 1976

JAY, Wally
Small-Circle Jujitsu
Ohara Publications
Burbank, CA 1989

MOTOBU, Choki
Okinawa Kempo Karate-Jutsu
tr. Seiyu Oyata
Ryukyu Imports
Olathe, KS 1977

NAGAMINE, Shoshin
The Essence of Okinawan Karate-do
Charles E. Tuttle
Rutland, Vermont 1976

NAKAYAMA, Masatoshi
Best Karate, Vol. 5 Heian, Tekki
Kodansha International, Ltd.
Tokyo, Japan, 1979

NETTER, Frank H., M.D.
Atlas of Human Anatomy
CIBA-GEIGY Ltd.
Basle, Switzerland, 1989

OHASHI, Wataru
Do-It-Yourself Shiatsu
E.P. Dutton
New York, 1976

OHASHI, Wataru with MONTE, Tom
**Reading the Body: Ohashi's Book of
Oriental Diagnosis**
Arcana Books
New York, 1991

SHANDONG MEDICAL COLLEGE &
SHANDONG COLLEGE OF TRADITIONAL
CHINESE MEDICINE
**Anatomical Atlas of Chinese
Acupuncture Points**
Pergamon Press for Shandong Science and
Technology Press
Elmsford, New York, 1982

SHANGHAI COLLEGE OF
TRADITIONAL MEDICINE
Acupuncture a Comprehensive Text
tr. John O'Connor & Dan Bensky
Eastland Press
Seattle, 1981

SHUM, Leung
Eagle Claw Kung Fu
Leung Shum
New York, 1980

THOMAS, Chris
**"Will Dillman's Tactics Work
on the Streets?"**
Inside Kung Fu, Oct. '89

**"Karate's Conspiracy of Silence:
Do Deadly Pressure Point Strikes Rea
Exist in Karate Kata?"**
Black Belt, Jan. '90

**"George Dillman Fights Back!
Controversial Karateka Answers
His Critics"**
Black Belt, Apr. '91

"Kata in Ryukyu Kempo"
Karate Kung-Fu Illustrated, Oct. '91

"Principles of Meaningful Kata"
Karate International, May '92

**"Reclaiming the Role of Kata: George
Dillman's Exciting Insights into
Traditional Karate"**
Combat, Sept. '92

**"Safe Pressure-Point Practice:
Safeguards and Resuscitation Method
for 'Death Touch' Training"**
Black Belt, Mar. '93

"Kata Centered Karate"
Fighting Arts International, No. 75

UESHIBA, Morihei
**Budo: Teachings of the Founder
of Aikido**
Kodansha International
Tokyo, 1991

WILSON-PAUWELS • AKESSON • STEWART
**Cranial Nerves: Anatomy and
Clinical Comments**
B. C. Decker, Inc.
Philadelphia, 1988